In the
Royal Manner

In the
Royal
Manner

Expert Advice on Etiquette
and Entertaining from
the Former Butler to Diana,
Princess of Wales

PAUL BURRELL

WARNER BOOKS

A Time Warner Company

For Maria, Alexander and Nicholas,
who make my life complete

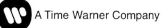 A Time Warner Company

Printed and bound in Great Britain by
Butler & Tanner Limited, Frome and London

First Printing: November 1999

10 9 8 7 6 5 4 3 2

ISBN: 0-446-52641-X
LCCN: 99-64432

Photography by Simon Smith,
assisted by Christopher Morris
Food styling by Kathryn Hawkins,
assisted by Sally Prong
Photographic styling by Clare Louise Hunt
Food historian Joan P Alcock
Book design by DW Design

Contents

FOREWORD

*D*URING MY TWENTY-TWO YEARS OF SERVICE to the Queen and the Duke of Edinburgh, and the Prince and Princess of Wales, I have been fortunate to witness the ultimate in stylish and elegant entertaining, from private and intimate family occasions at Sandringham and Highgrove to grand and lavish State Banquets for presidents, kings and queens. My memories of such events have led me to write this book, and share with you my experiences.

My upbringing was a far cry from the luxury of Buckingham Palace. I was born into an ordinary working-class family and lived in a small terraced house in the village of Grassmoor, a coal-mining community in the north of England. I vividly remember visiting London for the first time with my family when I was eight years old. Over the years I have often been reminded that while watching the Changing of the Guard at Buckingham Palace, I turned to my parents and said, 'One day I'm going to work here.'

However, it was not until recently that I discovered that it was my mother who chose my destiny, for which I will always be grateful. At her funeral, standing by her graveside, my younger brother turned to me and said, 'There is something you should know, Paul...'

He told me of an incident which had happened many years previously, while I was away at college. I had asked my mother to open all my mail during my absence. Two letters arrived on the same day, one bearing the Royal crest and offering me a position as a footman in the Royal household, the other from Cunard offering me a position as steward on board the *QEII*. Fearing that I might choose a life at sea, my mother burned the letter from Cunard on the coal fire, swearing my brother to secrecy for the rest of her life. It was a very poignant moment.

And so it was that at the age of eighteen I joined the staff of Buckingham Palace as a household footman, and my new life and career began.

After only a year, I became the Queen's personal footman, and soon began travelling with her and Prince Philip to almost every corner of the world. My experiences of Royal tours will remain with me for the rest of my life. From walking along the Great Wall of China with the Queen, to a visit to the remote South Pacific Island of Tuvalu aboard the Royal Yacht *Britannia*, or a visit to the Tutankhamun exhibition in Cairo with the Princess of Wales – each tour was unique and holds very special memories.

On one official visit to Saudi Arabia the Sultan's advisers ushered me into a cupboard in the Royal apartments before the Sultan and the Queen arrived. Apparently it was not protocol for staff to be in the Royal presence. Imagine Her Majesty's surprise when she had occasion to open the cupboard door, only to find me inside looking totally bemused!

On all our visits we were treated to sumptuous banquets where exotic foods such as truffles and caviar would be served on the finest china and silver. However, in complete contrast and in line with local traditions and customs, we were also encouraged to sample the more acquired taste of delicacies – the most memorable being sheep's eyes and monkey's brains served on banana leaves and coconut palms.

Entertaining in the Royal Household was more conventional. I attended and participated in the organization of Her Majesty's State Banquets and receptions for world leaders and heads of state, including the visits of President and Mrs Reagan at Windsor Castle, and the visit of his Holiness Pope John Paul II at Buckingham Palace.

her tragic death in the late summer of 1997.

My career within the Royal Households was extraordinary. I was given so many opportunities to see the world and experience situations which I could otherwise have only imagined. I poured vintage wines into crystal glasses, served delicious food from silver platters on to fine bone china, and decorated rooms and tables with beautiful flowers.

As recognition of my service to the Royal Family, I was decorated by the Queen with the Royal Victorian Medal at an investiture at Buckingham Palace in November 1997. I will treasure this proud moment, which I shared with my family, for the rest of my life, in the knowledge that I am the only person to have been awarded the RVM for services to Diana, Princess of Wales.

With this book, I will take you on a guided tour throughout the year and show you new ways of entertaining for every season and almost every situation. It is an honour to share with you my personal insights and unique knowledge, which I hope will eliminate all the stress and formality from entertaining. It is my sincere wish that you will enjoy entertaining with style.

In 1987, I was asked by the Prince and Princess of Wales to join their household at Highgrove House in Gloucestershire. I became butler to the most famous couple in the world and was responsible for their private entertaining both at home and abroad, and on official and private visits. Five years later, when the Royal couple sadly separated, the Princess was asked to compile a list of everything she would wish to take from Highgrove to her apartment at Kensington Palace. Much later I learned that at the top of her 'wish list' was my name.

For me, the Princess was the personification of style, and it was my privilege to serve and know such a unique and inspirational human being. From her I learnt that simplicity is often the most tasteful and attractive approach to entertaining. I remained in her service until

INTRODUCTION

Style is not the exclusive preserve of the rich and famous. Style can be achieved by anyone and is often most effective when simply executed. We all entertain; it may be as simple as inviting a friend for lunch or dinner at home, as special as a family gathering at Christmas, a christening or a wedding, or as challenging as a children's party. Whether we entertain on a simple level or with lavish flair depends on our individual style and how we want to show our hospitality, and also on the strength of our budget. So it is very important to plan your entertaining properly, and I will take you through the steps to ensure that your party is a success.

First, have a clear idea of the kind of event you want to hold, and who you would like to invite. This is the best way of working out how much it is going to cost and, of course, the numbers you will be catering for. The budget is obviously a great consideration for us all.

Once you have decided on the format of your party, you are then ready to send out the invitations. Make sure you clearly state the venue address, the time of arrival and any dress code (if appropriate). Printed invitations are necessary for formal events, but for a casual 'at home' or a family get-together a simple telephone call will suffice. Always mention the dress code – there is nothing more embarrassing than arriving at a function in the wrong clothes.

Remember that the names printed on invitations are the only people invited, so the names of partners and children should be included if you intend them to come along as well. When planning your invitations be sure to include an RSVP (*répondez, s'il vous plaît* – please

reply) and a contact address or telephone number, so that your guest can indicate, as soon as possible, whether they will be able to attend. It is polite to reply to an invitation within a week.

As far as timing is concerned, lunch is usually prompt at 1pm, in order to allow your guests time for other appointments later in the day. Dinner, although a formal meal, is often more relaxed, and is usually served between 8 and 9pm. It is polite and customary to invite your guests for a drink before dinner, and you need to specify this on the invitation: e.g. 8 for 8.30pm or 8.30 for 9pm.

Pre-dinner drinks and cocktails are an excellent opportunity for your guests to relax and get to know each other, especially if they have not met before. Choosing the right mix of people is an important factor in making your party a success, so do give some thought to choosing personalities who might mix well; there is nothing more boring than a room full of people who have little in common.

With these things covered, it is time to plan the menu and table setting. Remember to take into account any special dietary requirements and compile a list of drinks which you wish to serve during the course of your event. You should then check that you have enough china, glass, cutlery and serving utensils.

I have compiled the following guide to help you in choosing china, glass and tableware, setting the table, planning your menu and drinks, and choosing flowers for decorating your home and table. Remember that presentation is of the utmost importance.

PLANNING A DINNER PARTY

CHINA

Most of us have one good china dinner service which can be used for almost any occasion. An average service usually comprises of eighteen pieces: six each of main, side and sweet plates. The sweet plate can double as a first-course plate if you wish, although it is perfectly acceptable to use an entirely different set of plates for the sweet course. It can be very attractive, unusual and a talking point to use a collection of mis-matched but similar-sized plates for the sweet course. For example, a range of blue and white china of various designs or perhaps plates decorated with a common theme, such as animals or flowers. Use your imagination and individuality.

You may also find it useful to invest in a breakfast service which contains larger cups, saucers and side plates for that special brunch or breakfast tray in bed.

This selection of particularly decorative yet stylish plates gives a good example of the designs available. From left to right: limited edition, Asprey, London; Red Derby Panel by Royal Crown Derby, made exclusively for Asprey, London; hand-painted Limoges, Asprey, London; Green Derby Panel by Royal Crown Derby; Constance by Bernardaud; Eugénie by Thomas Goode.

GLASSWARE

We all have an assorted collection of glassware, most of which can be utilized for pre-dinner drinks or at the table. However, it is essential to have some uniformity at the place settings on your table. It has often been said that 'size isn't important' but in this instance it most definitely is. Traditionally, each drink should be served in a different style and different size of glass.

The essentials for a lunch or dinner party are a water glass and a wine glass (if you are serving red and white wine then you should have a different glass for each). Champagne should be served in a flute or champagne saucer or coupe. The flute is by far the most popular design because its shape helps maintain the champagne's sparkle.

I prefer clear crystal glassware with very little design as this looks more stylish. I would particularly choose glasses that are 'tulip' in shape, more bulbous at the bottom and slightly narrower at the top. Glasses should never be filled more than two thirds full. Red wine glasses are only filled one third full, to allow the aroma and flavour of the wine to develop. It is a personal preference whether red wine or water should be served in the largest glass.

| *Water / red wine* | *Red wine / water* | *Champagne* | *White wine* | *Sherry* | *Liqueur* |

BRANDY

Brandy is served in a 'balloon' glass which allows the brandy to breathe and reach room temperature more quickly: the larger the balloon, the quicker this will happen. I have served brandy in glasses as large as goldfish bowls – these are excellent for the brandy but they are a complete

nightmare to wash up afterwards!
The balloon should be cupped between both hands, and the brandy swirled gently around the glass before drinking. This will help you enjoy the beautiful aroma of this unique spirit as it warms and breathes. Port and Madeira can be served in a traditional sherry glass, or a smaller, tulip-shaped glass.

CUTLERY

A shortage of cutlery is probably the most common problem when entertaining. It is essential (but all too easy to forget) to check before your event that there are enough knives, forks and spoons available to accommodate each individual place setting. Remember that two sets of teaspoons will be needed if you are serving sorbets and coffee.

An ideal wedding present for anyone would be a canteen of cutlery, be it silver-plated or good-quality

| *Fiddle Thread* | *Raised Rattail* | *Albany* | *King's Royal* | *Louis XIV* | *Ribbons + bows* |

stainless steel. It will last a lifetime and will be invaluable for entertaining. Neither soup spoons nor fish knives and forks are fashionable these days, having been replaced in many homes with perfectly acceptable dessert spoons and smaller knives and forks. However if you have fish knives and soup spoons, by all means use them.

TABLE DRESSING

If you want to entertain with style and impress your guests, it is important to dress the table correctly. A well-polished table or a tablecloth is perfectly acceptable for either dinner or lunch. Personally, I prefer a lunch table to be set with a cloth, and a dinner table to remain uncovered with a rich, smooth polished surface upon which the candlelight can be reflected. But there is no definitive ruling, so it's up to your individual taste.

A standard table setting would consist of the following for each person:

A table mat
Cutlery for each course
A side plate and butter knife
Glasses for each wine served plus a glass
for water

You will also need a cruet of salt, pepper and mustard, usually shared, and a butter dish (optional).

If you have guests who smoke, remember to provide ashtrays when coffee is served. Some guests may wish to smoke throughout the meal and this is entirely at the host's discretion.

Forks are placed on the left-hand side of the place setting, and knives on the right. The spoon and fork for dessert may be placed either nearest the table mat or, alternatively, at the top of the place setting. Set the butter knife horizontally at the top of the side plate. The butter dish may be placed above the butter knife and the side plate.

A side plate should be placed on the left hand side of the place setting to use for bread and butter. (A roll should be broken in half and then into smaller pieces and buttered individually. Don't be afraid of making crumbs.)

If salad is to be served, it can be placed directly on to the main-course plate if the main course is cold. If the meal is hot then a separate salad plate or bowl should be provided for each person. This should be placed at the top left-hand corner of the place setting. The traditional crescent salad plate would be placed between the main-course plate and the salad plate, curving inwards. Salad can then be transferred from this plate on to the main-course plate before eating.

Throughout our history, a dessert service has been presented after the sweet plate has been cleared from the table. A typical service consists of a plate (fine porcelain and highly decorative), a napkin (often lace or embroidered), a knife, fork and spoon and a small glass finger bowl containing water fragranced with lemon or rose petals. I have seen foreign dignitaries, ambassadors and Members of Parliament drink the water from the finger bowl, and even put their fruit, sugar and cream in it to create their own fruit soup! It can be quite alarming to be presented with a dessert service for the first time but the host sets an example to those in any doubt!

Apart from the place settings, it is important for your table to have a central element. At lunch, it might consist of a simple arrangement of flowers which could incorporate vegetables and fruits as well. Dinner, however, is a more formal meal; a beautiful floral arrangement of seasonal flowers and foliage would be appropriate for the middle of the table, perhaps flanked or surrounded by candelabra or candlesticks. Don't make your arrangement too high – you want your guests to be able to see each other and converse across the table without being distracted by a 'forest' of flowers and candles.

NAPKINS

Although you can use any colour of napkin to suit your chosen colour theme, white will give you the most elegant appearance. There is no substitute for large, starched white linen napkins – they fold well and stand proud at any table setting. Although expensive, they will last for ever and will never go out of fashion – trust me.

Paper napkins are particularly suitable for a children's party, picnic or casual buffet, but not appropriate for a lunch or dinner party.

The folded napkin should stand in the centre of each place setting. I avoid placing napkins on side plates unless the first course is already on the table when your guests sit down. I have chosen to illustrate two of the most classic and stylish folded napkin arrangements.

PRINCE OF WALES' FEATHERS
'Fleur de Lys'

1. Fold your square napkin into a triangle and bring the left- and right-hand corners towards the top corner.
2. Fold the resulting diamond in half, from bottom to top, and then fold towards you, in half again.
3. Turn the napkin over and once again bring the left- and right-hand corners together and tuck in.
4. Stand the napkin upright and peel down the two side folds.
5. Finally, peel down the top corner.

1.

2.

3.

4.

5.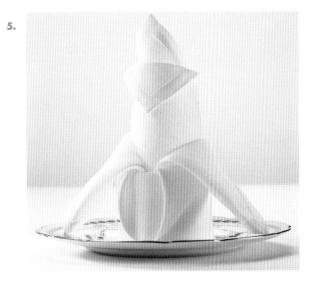

5.

SYDNEY OPERA HOUSE
'Cock's Comb'

1. Fold your square napkin into quarters, making sure that all four corners are together.
2. Fold the bottom corner into the top corner, turn the napkin over, then fold the left- and right-hand corners towards the centre.
3. Tuck the two loose flaps underneath.
4. Fold in half once again to make a 'boat' shape, then pull the four corners up for the 'sails'.
5. Now you have a perfect Sydney Opera House or Cock's Comb.

1.

2.

3.

4.

TABLE LINEN TIPS

• If you scorch a white cotton napkin, wet the mark with soapy water and leave it to dry in bright sunlight. Wash and iron it again, and the scorch will disappear.

• Freshly washed white linen can be hung overnight in a heavy frost to help restore the crisp whiteness, as if by magic!

SEATING

You will already have an idea where you wish your guests to sit at the table, but here are a few basic guidelines you might like to consider. As a general rule, the most important guest should sit on the right of the host, and their partner should sit on the right side of the hostess. When appropriate, you should try to alternate men and women, otherwise a good starting point is for you to sit opposite your partner.

If you are entertaining more than six guests, a table plan is a good idea and avoids unnecessary confusion when your guests approach the table, or you can write place cards. At a smaller party, you can simply direct your guests to their seats.

PAUL'S THREE GOLDEN RULES
OF SUCCESSFUL ENTERTAINING

1 RELAX
and have fun – after all, that's what entertaining is all about!

2 RESIST
anything too adventurous, extravagant or expensive.

3 KEEP IT SIMPLE
because simplicity is often the most stylish principle.

CHOOSING A MENU

This is often the most difficult task, and you must give clear and careful thought to choosing your menu. Three courses are customary, although sorbets and water ices can be introduced to cleanse the palette between courses, and a fish course could be introduced if appropriate. However, it would be foolish to attempt anything too elaborate unless you are very experienced; by all means be adventurous, but don't overstretch yourself.

Think about who you are inviting and what their tastes are. Spicy, hot food can be a culture shock for some people: for example, many people don't like curries. You should also take into account anyone who is vegetarian, or who has food allergies or is on a special diet. Aim for a good balance of colours, textures and flavours; make the meal look pleasing to the eye. There is nothing more attractive than the simple elegance of a dish of freshly cooked baby carrots or new potatoes.

The first course or starter, a simple introduction to what will follow, could consist of either soup, fruit, fish or a vegetable appetizer. This will be followed by the more substantial main course, usually meat- or fish-based and often served with a selection of vegetables or salad.

The sweet, or 'pudding' as it is known in the Royal Household, would be served next. Whereas hearty steamed puddings and pies served with custard would be offered at lunchtime, at dinner it is wiser to choose lighter dishes such as Pears in Port Wine with Cinnamon Ice Cream (see page 97). Cheese would follow. Although cheese and fruit should always be served at lunchtime, some people decide against serving cheese in the evening unless it is a rich cheese such as Stilton, accompanied by port.

SELECTING THE DRINKS

Once you have decided on your menu, you can choose which drinks are to be served, especially pre-dinner drinks and cocktails. For an outdoor summer event, there's nothing more refreshing than a long, cool Pimm's cocktail, as traditionally served at Royal Ascot, Wimbledon and Royal Garden Parties. Iced tea and coffee have also become strong summer favourites.

Other cocktails and aperitifs are usually served before a dinner party – for some specific ideas and recipes, see pages 140 – 141. Gin and tonic, whisky and sherry are customary pre-dinner drinks; the latter can also be served with consommé – a light clear soup – as a first course. Sherry and port served with ice are also becoming quite popular, while a light or sparkling wine is always an excellent choice to offer your guests.

Champagne can be rather expensive, but a cheaper sparkling white wine can be livened up by adding freshly squeezed orange juice to make a Buck's Fizz, or try adding a dash of the blackcurrant liqueur, Cassis, to champagne to make a Kir Royale.

To accompany the meal itself, full-bodied clarets and red wines are served with rich meals, red meat and game, and fruity crisp white wines such as Moselle or Chardonnay to accompany lighter dishes such as fish or chicken. Vintage and good-quality red wine must be opened at least two hours before serving, decanted and allowed to breathe and reach room temperature. Beaujolais, white and rosé wines, sparkling wine and champagne should be served chilled. I have suggested a few wines to go with some recipes in this book, which you may find a useful reference.

Make sure there is plenty of iced mineral water available throughout the meal for your guests, and don't forget to cater for those who don't drink alcohol.

You may want to serve a dessert wine with the sweet course, and you should make sure that this is very cold. After the sweet, you may choose to serve port with cheese, biscuits and fruit. The port should be decanted and is traditionally passed clockwise around the table. Other liqueurs aren't really necessary and

bottles often sit untouched in cupboards until the next dinner party. If you want to offer something other than port, then brandy is the best alternative.

Coffee and tea are served at the end of the meal, and it is worth remembering that some people prefer decaffeinated or herbal teas – chamomile and peppermint are generally popular. The Princess preferred a brew of grated ginger root steeped in hot water, which has particular cleansing and detoxifying properties, and is good for settling the stomach.

WINE

There is much snobbery attached to wine, and most of us feel out of our depth when presented with a very long wine list or faced with endless rows of bottles in the local wine store. The main thing to bear in mind is that drinking wine should be an enjoyable and pleasurable pastime. Experienced wine-tasters often use terms like 'bubble gum', 'biscuity','nutty' and even 'petrolly' when describing their favourite vintages, but please don't be alarmed by these descriptive words. Be confident in your own taste and sample different wines, as this way you will learn what is most appealing to *you* and your palette.

As a general rule, wine should look clear. However, older wines especially red varieties may contain sediment and will need decanting before serving. One of the simplest ways to choose the right wine with the particular characteristics that you like is to look at the label and recognize the grape variety.

WHITE WINES

CHARDONNAY An easy variety of grape to grow and one which produces the most popular and fashionable of wines, Chardonnay grapes grow all round the world. Some familiar names might be

White Burgundy, Chablis, Meursault and Montrachet. The latter is one of my favourite white wines, and one which is versatile enough to serve throughout a meal. It is often aged in oak barrels and has a distinctive dry, vanilla taste. Serve this crisp, clear wine to accompany richer fish and white meat dishes, or simply enjoy its unique qualities as a pre-dinner aperitif.

GEWÜRZTRAMINER I associate this grape with Germany as *Gewürz* in German means spice, although it is also produced in other countries. The German wine is bottled in tall, brown, slim bottles, and tastes full and fruity. It may be too fruity and sweet for those who prefer the drier Chardonnay. This wine would typically be served at lunches or with the first course at a dinner. Try serving it with the Rosemary Bread Cases with Fennel and Egg Fricassee recipe on page 122, or with the Victorian Dinner on pages 92.

MUSCADET The Muscadet grape lends its name to a classic wine which is grown almost exclusively in the Nantes region of the French Loire Valley. It is very dry, light and crisp with little 'bouquet', and it is drunk whilst young. Ideal to accompany plain fish and white meat dishes, or enjoy as an early evening refreshment.

MUSCAT This grape is grown throughout the wine regions of the world and is associated with sweet, sticky, rich after-dinner wines. It should be served as cold as possible to accompany puddings and sweets. The honeyed French Muscats of Beaumes de Venise are probably the most famous example. Perfect to serve with the Tipsy Ratafia Trifle on page 126, or the Pears in Port Wine with Cinnamon Ice Cream on page 97.

RIESLING This sweet wine is bottled similarly to Gewürztraminer. It has a musky aroma and a citrus aftertaste. Serve with plain fish and white meat dishes.

SAUVIGNON BLANC Generally produces a dry, crisp fruity wine with a sharp acidity. Famous examples include the group of French wines Sancerre and Pouilly-Fumé. Ideal to serve with rich fish and white meat dishes. Try it with the Small Fishcakes with Lemon and Sorrel Sauce on pages 92 – 93.

RED WINES

CABERNET SAUVIGNON Most famous of all red grapes, grown worldwide. The wine produced is medium to full-bodied and inky red in colour. It is an excellent accompaniment to spiced rich red meats with sauces or gravy. The best clarets in the world are made from this grape and the wine is aged in oak barrels for 15 – 20 years. This gives a spicy, vanilla flavour to the wine. The aroma is unmistakably that of blackcurrants. Ideal with the Roast Beef on page 94.

MERLOT Famous in the Bordeaux region of France, well-known Merlot wines include St. Emilion and Pomerol. It is successfully grown in many other regions of the world as well. A wine-taster would describe this wine as having a chocolaty aftertaste, and a perfumed sweet aroma. Perfect served with the Roast Beef.

GAMAY An unfamiliar name perhaps, but a very well-known wine: Beaujolais Nouveau. Light, bubble-gum-flavoured wine which is drunk young. Try serving this chilled with the Crown Roast of Lamb on page 52.

PINOT NOIR This grape produces Red Burgundy, and is full bodied with an aroma of raspberries and strawberries. A perfect complement to most red meat dishes.

SYRAH/SHIRAZ This grape produces a dark, full-bodied, inky wine from northern regions in France, Australia and South Africa. It has a rich plum flavour. In Australia it is called Shiraz. Serve with spiced rich red meat casseroles and stews, or meat dishes with sauces.

Always serve champagne well chilled, and when opening a bottle do not prise the cork, but gently turn the bottle with one hand whilst releasing the cork with the other. Take care as a cork can fly out at a tremendous speed and could seriously injure an unsuspecting guest!

UNCORKING WINE

You will need a sharp knife to cut away the foil or plastic from just below the lip of the bottle before you attempt to remove the cork. The many corkscrew devices on the market mostly use a screw-pull action which is intended to extract the cork whole.

The extraction of a cork from a fine vintage port, claret or wines over seven years old can be more difficult as the corks usually disintegrate. These wines should be filtered through fine muslin into a decanter or claret jug.

DECANTING WINE

Ideally, good-quality red wine should have been stored in a horizontal position to allow the sediment to settle. Therefore I would suggest that you leave the bottle upright, undisturbed, for two days before opening. Gently pull the cork and, using some fine muslin (or a coffee filter paper) and a funnel, slowly pour the contents of the bottle into the decanter or claret jug. If you do this with a light behind the flow of the wine, you will see that as little sediment as possible escapes from the bottle. There should be little waste, although some is inevitable. Once decanted, the wine should be clear, and left to stand for about two hours to reach room temperature.

I prefer clarets and other red wines to be served warmer, as it gives a much richer and fuller flavour to the wine. White, rosé, sparkling and dessert wines are generally served chilled (but avoid putting them in a freezer in order to chill them down quickly, as this will alter the taste of the wine). By far the most effective way to cool wine quickly is to put the bottles in buckets of iced water.

CHAMPAGNE

This is *the* celebratory drink and is the most famous wine in the world. It has no rival. It is impressive and ultimately the most stylish drink. Recently, I attended a reception to celebrate the marriage of Asprey & Garrard, the Crown Jewellers, where we were served tiny bottles of champagne with a straw – a novel and very stylish way to serve the drink, and so simply executed.

At a formal dinner party champagne or dessert wine such as Château d'Yquem or Beaumes de Venise would be served with the sweet dish. Genuine champagne comes from the Champagne region of France and nowhere else. It was the Romans who originally established the vineyards in the chalky soils of this particular corner of France, only 100 miles from Paris. The church continued to tend the vines and a monk called Dom Perignon is widely recognized as the person who invented the champagne cork and cage which traps the bubbles inside the bottle.

MIND YOUR MANNERS, PLEASE

OR, THE ART OF BEING THE PERFECT GUEST

Imagine now that you are going to a party. I have compiled this guide around common etiquette dos and don'ts. Some are more obvious, but others I'm sure will surprise you.

It is advisable to be punctual at an engagement, although it is acceptable to be 10 minutes late, but no more. Traffic and taxis can delay and hamper anyone's arrival though. If you want to take someone with you to the event, it is common courtesy to check with your host beforehand. (If you are hosting a party, and one of your guests brings a friend, there is nothing you can do about it other than to greet them warmly, then address the situation with your inconsiderate guest at a later date.) It is polite to take along a small gift for the host or hostess such as flowers, after dinner chocolates, wine or champagne. I have often found a perfumed candle to be a guaranteed success.

There are a few basic rules which should be observed at any dining table.

- Unfold your napkin once you are seated and place it on your lap, and use it to wipe your mouth and fingers during the meal. At the end of the meal it is polite to leave the napkin tidily on the place setting – not scrunched up on the floor!
- The host will always give you a clear indication of when to start the meal. They may begin with a few words of welcome, or Grace, and traditionally the lady sitting on the right of the host is served first, then the rest of the table in a clockwise direction.
- A knife and fork should be held with the handles in the palm of the hand, forefinger on top, and thumb underneath. Forks should not be turned over unless tackling peas, rice, sweetcorn kernels, or suchlike, in which case transfer the fork to the right hand. At an informal meal, buffet or barbecue, it is of course perfectly acceptable to eat with just a fork.

- It is unwise to use your bread to mop up sauces, although this is customary in other parts of Europe.
- A sweet can be eaten with a spoon and fork, or just a fork if it is of cake-like consistency.
- Rest your knife and fork in between mouthfuls by leaning the knife and fork on the edge of the plate. Only when you have finished should you place them side by side in the centre of the plate.

Should your host present a completely inedible dish, I would suggest that the best course of action is to at least make some attempt at disguising your disgust: cut it up and move it around your plate a little – perhaps no one will notice. More obviously slurping, burping, picking teeth and licking fingers are particularly unattractive, although it is acceptable to pick up meat on the bone such as chicken legs and spare ribs. It is the only way to eat them. Have a napkin and finger bowl on standby for messy fingers.

Remember that you haven't been invited to dinner just to eat, the evening would be more enjoyable if you made polite conversation, however small, to those sitting on your right and left, and make sure you give both sides equal attention. Don't talk with your mouth full or sit with your elbows on the table.

AFTER DINNER

Throughout Victorian and Edwardian England, it was customary for the ladies to retire to the drawing room after the dessert had been served. The ladies would then play a card game such as canasta or bridge, and wait for the gentlemen to join them. The men would gather at the end of the dining table and drink brandy and port, smoke, and discuss business and tell stories. This is still common practice in the Royal Household.

HOW TO EAT DIFFICULT FOOD

Impress your friends by tackling awkward and difficult food with confidence and professionalism! I have listed below a selection of notoriously difficult foods and suggest how I might tackle them:

ARTICHOKES Take off the leaves one at a time using your fingers, and dip the fleshy base of each leaf into the sauce provided. Strip off the flesh with your teeth and discard the rest on the edge of your plate. The leaves near the heart have no flesh. Eventually, the centre core will be exposed, then scrape away the 'thistle' at the base and eat the rest with a knife and fork.

ASPARAGUS Pick up each spear with your fingers and dip it in the sauce provided. There should be at least two bites before you get to the woody end – do not eat the last 5cm/2in of the stem – place the end of the stem on the side of your plate, *not* the side plate.

CAVIAR & TOAST Using a small knife, lightly cover the end of the toast with caviar. Sometimes, caviar is served in small pots, in which case it should be eaten with a teaspoon.

CHEESE Never cut the tip off a wedge of cheese. Cut along the length, leaving the wedge in a similar shape. Use a hard steel-bladed knife for cutting hard cheese, and a smaller knife for soft cheese.

CORN ON THE COB Not the easiest food to eat in public. Small handles may have been provided at either end of the sweetcorn, thus enabling you to nibble away like a mouse! Otherwise pick up with your fingers. Have a napkin on hand for the dripping butter.

CRAB The meat will have been dressed and replaced in the shell. The claws may be served along with a nutcracker-style tool to crack them open, and a metal pick with which to pull out the meat from within the cavities.

LOBSTER Normally presented to you cut in half lengthways. The most difficult aspect of eating lobster is extracting the flesh from the claw. You will be provided with the correct implement to do this. It is a messy business, you should also be provided with an extra napkin and a finger bowl.

MUSSELS Usually you will be presented with a mountain of mussel shells, gaping open to reveal small orangy pieces of meat. Take a large shell and use it like a pair of tweezers to pull out the mussels from their shells. A separate bowl will be provided for the empty shells. You can use a fork if you prefer. Use a spoon to eat the remaining stock.

OYSTERS Squeeze lemon juice over the raw oyster, then use a small fork to detach it from its anchor and 'drink' the oyster from its shell.

PRAWNS (WHOLE) Pull off the head, detaching it from its shoulders. Turn over and peel away the shell, removing the egg sac and legs. The tail shell will detach easily and you will be left with the body to eat. A finger bowl and napkin will be provided for you to freshen your fingers.

SOUP Push the spoon away from you and sip from the spoon. Always tip the bowl away from you, and never put the whole spoon in your mouth.

SPAGHETTI Spear a fork into the spaghetti, and twist it round until a ball begins to form. As you eat from the fork, bite off all residual strands, letting them fall back on to the plate – you may want to use a spoon as well to help you.

WHITEBAIT These little fish are cooked whole and eaten just as they are – eyeballs included!

HOW TO EAT FRESH FRUIT

APPLE Cut into quarters, core and peel each piece individually.

BANANA Cut off the ends with your knife, then split the skin and peel it away with your fingers. Cut into small pieces with your dessert knife and fork to eat.

CHERRIES Remove the stalk, eat whole and remove the stone discreetly between your thumb and forefinger.

KIWI FRUIT Split in half widthwise and scoop out the flesh using a teaspoon.

ORANGE Score the skin in a segment fashion and remove the skin. Eat in segments.

PEAR Split in half lengthwise, then quarter, core and peel if necessary. If a pear is particularly ripe, try cutting it in half horizontally and scooping out the flesh with a teaspoon.

Manners and etiquette matter a great deal, and are as important now as they ever were. Here are some more common courtesy hints and tips which you can adapt to different circumstances.

Smoking is widely unfashionable nowadays, so when amongst a group of people, it is polite to ask if anyone objects to you 'lighting up', especially when dining. Try to avoid blowing smoke in another person's direction. If you are the host, it is perfectly acceptable for you to object to anyone smoking within the house, and to ask your guests to refrain from doing so.

At the end of a meal, ladies may want to apply a little powder or lipstick. It is appropriate to do this at the table, but major repair works should be carried out in the ladies' room!

Should you be cornered by a boring person at a party, then the most common excuse would be to ask where the lavatory is, and make a quick exit. Otherwise, you could spot someone in the room you 'really must speak to', excuse yourself politely and then leave, or introduce them to someone else before excusing yourself.

A well-known media personality holds the record for the fastest-ever lunch at Kensington Palace. He was entertained and despatched within 60 minutes. His crime? He simply bored the Princess.

Sometimes one-to-one lunches can be rather restricting, so try to include friends among your guests.

I have always been told not to be the last person to leave a party. Unfortunately sometimes it is inevitable. However, it is considered to be good manners to leave while 'the night is still young'! If someone refuses to leave your party, then could I suggest that you subtly ask them if they would like a drink before they leave, or whether you can order them a taxi.

It is very important to remember to write to your hosts and thank them for inviting you to their party. You will probably be in the minority, but you will stand out from the crowd and make a good impression.

The Princess would often say that people didn't say thank you enough, yet it is those two words which can mean so much. With strict discipline, she would spend hours at her writing table penning thank-you notes for presents, luncheons, dinners and general kindnesses that

CARRIAGES

In Elizabethan England, chivalry meant that a gentleman would alight from the carriage first in order to help the ladies by offering them his hand or arm for stability. This tradition, alas, is now long gone, along with a gentleman walking on the roadside to protect his lady from splashing vehicles. However, it is still appropriate to hold a door open for a lady and to forfeit a seat on public transport, although I'll leave this as a personal choice as some ladies may find it condescending and offensive.

came her way. These notes would be handwritten and often delivered by hand on the same day. As preparation, before each engagement, the envelope would be written and then placed neatly on her desk to await its contents upon her return.

GUESTS TO STAY IN YOUR HOME

Attention to detail and a warm welcome are the most important elements when you invite people to stay with you. The information in this section is based on my experiences over many years, and is tried and tested. Although it applies mainly to larger households, you can easily adapt it to your own home.

Always check the guest room before your guests arrive. Check the lighting, a bedside table lamp is essential. Place a few interesting books or magazines for bedtime reading on the table. You would often find a Dick Francis, Jeffrey Archer, Mary Wesley or Catherine Cookson novel at the bedside in a Royal Household. If your guests smoke, then don't forget to provide them with an ashtray.

Make sure that extra blankets are to hand in case your guests get cold in the night. I have slept in many draughty rooms in castles and country houses and I know how unpleasant that can be. It is impossible to sleep once your temperature drops and you start shivering!

Place a small vase of flowers in the room to make it more welcoming and cheery, and a bottle of still mineral water with a glass should be placed in the bathroom. If your guests are sharing a bathroom, make sure they have adequate towels. If they have their own bathroom, then you could provide soap and bath oils. The Floris range of traditional floral fragrances have been long-time favourites with many members of the Royal Family.

Make sure that there is plenty of toilet tissue in the bathroom and a box of tissues on the dressing table is always very welcome. You may also wish to place a spare toothbrush, toothpaste, disposable razor and cottonwool balls in a small container in the bathroom.

Why not have a special visitors' book to record your

MISHAPS

Inevitably accidents do happen and things gets spilt from time to time. I have always found that the old-fashioned remedies are the best way to deal with common mishaps. Drinks getting knocked over is probably the most common problem at a party, but with prompt action they are easy to deal with:

Beer – mix a little ammonia in warm, soapy water and dab over the stain. Leave to dry and then wash as usual.

Coffee – it is important to deal with the stain quickly by soaking in cold water. Then rub with washing detergent and rinse out. You can use a mild bleach solution on white fabrics, but not coloured.

Red wine – mop stain immediately with an absorbent cloth, then sprinkle on salt and leave for five minutes to absorb wine, then wash as soon as possible.

Tea – soak in cold water for a few minutes, then in a borax and cold water solution before washing in hot, soapy water.

Dogs and cats around the home often have accidents. Dog puddles can stain carpets badly. You may find a bottle of soda water and blotting paper or toilet tissue invaluable. Pour the soda water on to the stain and allow time for it to soak into the carpet. Blot away immediately – the gas will help lift the stain from the carpet.

It is also useful to know how to get the marks off your table linen in order to keep it looking pristine each time you use it. Here are some techniques you may find useful:

Butter – soak up as much of the residue as possible with kitchen paper. Rub some washing detergent into the stain and then wash in hot, soapy water. If the fabric is unwashable, place blotting paper under the stain and dab with a little carbon tetrachloride.

Chocolate – sponge with borax solution and wash in warm, soapy water.

Egg – soak in cold, soapy water for a few minutes and wash as normal.

Lipstick – rub the stain with glycerine and leave for an hour and then wash in very hot, soapy water.

VALETS AND MAIDS

Traditionally in Royal Households and large country homes gentlemen would be allocated a valet and ladies a dresser or ladies' maid to unpack, press and wash clothes and to attend to their guests' personal requirements. Couples sharing the same room would be 'called' by their maid at a given time with a morning tray of tea, coffee or orange juice accompanied by the traditional Rich Tea or Digestive biscuit.

memorable events, especially when your guests stay overnight. It will be a valuable point of reference in years to come and a reminder of enjoyable times like anniversaries, birthdays and other family gatherings. A leather-bound book with the name of the residence or family embossed on the cover would make an ideal gift for any relative or friend who likes to entertain or for a wedding present. Each page can be dedicated to a particular event, with a list of guests who came along, the menu or any other appropriate information. You could then invite your guests to write a few words before they leave, or simply sign their name.

FLOWERS

It is very satisfying to walk down a country lane lined with flowering hedgerows. The fragrance and spectacle of living colour are very inspirational and uplifting. Flowers can help transform any occasion by setting the scene or by giving a beautiful backdrop.

During my career, I regularly filled rooms with the best-quality and freshest seasonal flowers available. I used to select them personally early each morning at the Covent Garden flower market. Simple glass vases of sweet peas, narcissi, parrot tulips and English roses were particular favourites of the Princess, as were planted baskets of hyacinths, snowdrops, lilies of the valley and primulas. Later in this book, you will find

ideas for displays to suit each season in step-by-step guides, making the most of my favourite flowers at the specific time of year. I aim to inspire you with these suggestions and hope that you will create your own displays for your home and dining table.

TIPS FOR LONG-LASTING ARRANGEMENTS

The preparation of flowers and greenery is very important in order to keep them for the longest time possible:

- For cut flowers, always recut the stem bases at a slant before submerging them in cold water. Stand them in a bucket of water, with cut flower food if possible, ideally overnight, to allow them to refresh before arranging.
- Woody stems such as roses should be cut on a slant and then crushed with a heavy weight.
- If you wish your blooms to open quickly, especially tight rosebuds, submerge the whole stems in tepid water for at least an hour.
- In floral arrangements, always remove leaves from the stems of flowers and greenery which are to be submerged in water.
- A drop of household bleach and a teaspoon of sugar or cut flower food will help keep the water and flowers fresh. Do not use bleach in conjunction with silver as it will tarnish it badly.

ROSES

These favourite flowers can be particularly unpredictable. Always choose roses with firm, tight centres and buds. You may find that their heads droop; this is due to air being trapped beneath the head of the rose. It can be corrected by pushing a pin through the stem at the base of the flower head. Recut the stems and plunge in boiling water for ten to fifteen seconds. Another remedy is lay the entire stem including the flower head in a tub of cold water for two hours.

To make this stunning arrangement see page 58 – 59.

Spring

SPRING

Winter's hard, cold grip thaws into a burst of new life and colour. Spring flowers bloom,

animals awake from hibernation and life begins afresh.

Kensington Palace Gardens are carpeted with bluebells, crocuses and snowdrops, providing a spectacular backdrop to the red-brick façade of the oldest of Royal residences in London, the Princess's home for over fifteen years. The Princess – whom I always affectionately called 'The Boss' – would take advantage of the 270 acres of wide open space, whether it be jogging, sitting under a tree reading a book or simply watching the world go by.

Each year on 1 March, St David's Day, I accompany a group of children from a leukaemia hospital in Llandough, South Wales, to lay daffodils, the national emblem of Wales, in memory of their Princess, at those now famous gates.

In this section, I have chosen the event of Easter as a main theme, as it is such a special and important time of the year. I have also included a romantic meal for two and a brunch menu – plenty of suggestions, I hope, to inspire your entertaining.

5.

1.

2.

3.

4.

SPRING VASE ARRANGEMENT

Fresh, clean and bright, this stunning vase of mixed green and yellow spring flowers will bring sunshine into any room. Trumpet-shaped fluted tulips fall naturally over a plain glass vase. Simple and elegant vases of flowers are often the most attractive of all arrangements. You can adjust the amount of flowers you use according to the size of your vase. Also, try small square or round vases of tightly packed lilies of the valley, narcissi and hyacinths.

Step 1

A few sprays of greenery such as eucalyptus

A bunch of bear grass

About 50 fluted tulips

2 bunches of Michaelmas daisies

About 20 stems of Veronica (speedwell)

1 large vase half full of water

Step 2

Build up a structure of greenery by working in a round, alternating leaves and grass. Hold the arrangement in one hand and feed with the other, until you have built up a basic frame for the flowers.

Step 3

Adding the tulips: trim the leaves and 5cm/2in from the base of each tulip – this will inhibit their growth. Working with about half of the tulips, feed them into the greenery, adding more grass if necessary, while turning the arrangement in your hand.

Step 4

Because tulips have fleshy stems you need to support them by adding stems of Michaelmas daisies and Veronica. Make sure you keep turning the arrangement to give an even balance of flowers and greenery.

Step 5

Finish off by pushing the remaining tulips into the arrangement where appropriate. Trim the stems with scissors and place in a vase. Rearrange any stems if necessary and top up with more water if needed.

ROMANTIC DINNER FOR TWO

Spoil your partner by preparing this simple, stylish and delicious romantic dinner – ideal for Valentine's Day or an intimate evening at home.

When preparing a romantic meal, concentrate on simple, familiar food, especially food that can be prepared in advance. Atmosphere is the essential element and any romantic setting would be incomplete without candlelight and music. Classical music can be wonderful in a romantic setting, as can popular love ballads. When organizing your table setting don't sit opposite each other, this is an evening to be together, so sit next to each other and enjoy a glass of your favourite wine or champagne.

The Princess's philosophy on entertaining was simple, easy and elegantly executed.

She fully understood that it was intimidating to be invited to a palace to meet a Princess for the first time. Her priority was to break down those pre-determined barriers and to provide her guests with a lasting memory of their special day.

The Princess would have instructed me to place small hand-tied bouquets of seasonal flowers on the seats of lady guests at the luncheon table. The men, not to be left out, would also receive small gifts of cufflinks or pocket notepads.

A warm welcome and an informal chat would often reassure guests that this was not an austere and formidable environment.

ITALIAN SALAD OF MOZZARELLA, AVOCADO AND TOMATO

A stylish starter. You'll be amazed by the Mediterranean flavours that will come through from a few simple ingredients.

Serves: 2
Preparation time: 15 minutes plus chilling
No cooking

1 small ripe avocado
Juice of 1 small lemon
4 ripe plum tomatoes
175g/6oz piece mozzarella cheese
50g/2oz pitted black olives
1 tbsp pesto sauce
1 tbsp olive oil
Salt and freshly ground black pepper
A few fresh basil leaves

1. Halve the avocado and remove the stone. Peel off the skin and slice the flesh thinly. Place in a bowl and sprinkle with the lemon juice.
2. Thinly slice the tomatoes and mozzarella. Gently toss into the avocado along with the olives. Cover and chill for 30 minutes.
3. Just before serving, drain the avocado, tomatoes, mozzarella and olives, reserving the juices, and pile on to serving plates.
4. Mix the reserved juices with the pesto sauce and olive oil and drizzle a little over each portion. Season and sprinkle with the basil leaves. Serve with the remaining dressing on the side.

BAKED SEA BASS IN FILO
WITH JULIENNE VEGETABLES

These beautifully packaged fillets of sea bass served on a bed of 'just-cooked' shredded vegetables are simple to prepare and look stunning. It's a meal in itself so you won't need to serve anything else with this course.

Serves: 2

Preparation time: 20 minutes plus cooling
Cooking time: approx. 30 minutes

65g/2½oz butter
75g/3oz button mushrooms, wiped and chopped
Salt and freshly ground black pepper
2 x 25g/1oz sheets filo pastry
2 x 150g/5oz skinless sea bass fillet steaks
2 tbsp freshly chopped parsley
175g/6oz carrot
175g/6oz courgette (zucchini)
1 small leek

Preheat the oven to 200° C/400° F/Gas 6

1. Melt 15g/½oz butter in a frying pan and gently fry the mushrooms for 2 – 3 minutes until just softened. Remove from the heat and season. Set aside to cool.

2. Melt half the remaining butter in a small saucepan. Lay the filo sheets out on the work surface and brush with melted butter. Fold each sheet over and brush again.

3. Lay a fish fillet in the centre of each, season and top each with some of the mushrooms and chopped parsley. Fold over two opposite corners of pastry and then bring up the other two to form a parcel, scrunching and twisting them together as they meet in the middle.

4. Press gently to seal and then transfer to a baking sheet. Brush with butter and bake for 20 – 25 minutes until crisp, golden and cooked through.

5. Meanwhile, peel the carrot and cut into very thin sticks, or coarsely grate. Trim the courgette (zucchini) and cut or grate in the same way. Trim the leek, slice in half lengthwise, and run under water to flush out any trapped earth. Shake well to remove excess water and then shred finely. Set aside.

6. Five minutes before the sea bass is cooked, melt the remaining butter and stir-fry the prepared vegetables for 2 – 3 minutes until just tender.

7. To serve, divide the shredded vegetables between two warmed serving plates and season. Top each pile of vegetables with a parcel of fish and serve with wedges of lemon to squeeze over.

Cook's note: to save even more time, look out for packs of ready-cut courgette and carrot 'en julienne' in your local supermarket.

TIRAMISU HEARTS

This traditional Italian dish was introduced to the Princess by an Italian chef who came to Kensington Palace from the world-famous Cipriani Hotel in Venice. It immediately became a favourite and for a while it seemed that everyone who came to lunch had tiramisu for pudding, long before this dessert became widely known outside Italy.

Serves: 2

Preparation time: 20 minutes plus chilling
No cooking

> 200g/7oz piece chocolate marble cake
> 1 tbsp cold, strong black coffee
> 4 tbsp brandy
> 200g/7oz tub medium-fat soft cheese
> 1 tsp vanilla essence
> 1 tbsp icing sugar
> 1 ripe mini mango
> 2 tsp cocoa powder
> White chocolate shavings and cape gooseberries to decorate

1. Line a 19 cm/7in square tin with clear wrap so that it overhangs the sides of the tin. Thinly slice the marble cake to fit the tin and press the slices side by side into the base of the tin. Mix the coffee with 2 tbsp brandy and sprinkle all over the cake.

2. In a mixing bowl, beat the soft cheese with the vanilla essence. Sift the icing sugar into the bowl and carefully mix.

3. Pile the cheese mixture on top of the soaked cake and spread evenly. Cover and chill for 30 minutes.

4. Meanwhile, peel the mango and slice down either side of the smooth, flat central stone. Chop the flesh and then place in a food processor or blender with the remaining brandy. Blend until smooth. Transfer to small bowl, cover and chill until required.

5. Carefully remove the cheese-covered cake from the tin by pulling up the clear wrap. Using a 7cm/3in heart-shaped cutter, stamp out four shapes from the cake.

6. Using a palette knife, lift each heart off the clear wrap and then stack one heart on top of another to make two thicker hearts. Dust the tops with a little cocoa.

7. Transfer each to a serving plate, decorate with white chocolate shavings, dust with more cocoa and serve with the mango coulis spooned around and cape gooseberries on the side.

Cook's note: don't waste the trimmings, they'll make a treat for the next day! To make chocolate shavings, melt the chocolate of your choice and spread it thickly on a board. Allow to set in the fridge and then remove and allow to reach room temperature. Using a cheese slicer, 'shave' off pieces of chocolate and place in the fridge until required.

APHRODISIAC FOODS

If you're planning a romantic meal for your loved one, then you might just be interested in choosing foods which are regarded as having aphrodisiac qualities. I am including a few suggestions for you to try:

SHELLFISH — the most commonly known aphrodisiac, with oysters and lobsters being top of the shellfish hot list.

CAVIAR — it is easy to eat and digest, and is perfect served with champagne.

SPICES — especially vanilla and cardamom.

TRUFFLES, FIGS AND POMEGRANATES — the latter reputedly being a fertility symbol.

CHOCOLATE — Casanova recommended this as an aphrodisiac!

NUTS — The Queen of Sheba favoured pistachio nuts as an aphrodisiac. And the Greeks and Romans scattered walnuts at marriage ceremonies and burned hazel torches as symbols of the newlyweds' fertility and future happiness together.

SPRING BRUNCH

This is an excellent way to guarantee Mum a lazy morning in bed. Some of the recipes here

are simple enough for children to prepare (with a little help perhaps). Make it special by

picking a few spring flowers from the garden for a surprise breakfast tray.

A tasty treat for Mother's Day

FRESH FRUIT PLATTER WITH FRUITS OF THE FOREST DIP

Serves: 4

Preparation time: 15 minutes

No cooking

1 baby pineapple

¼ small watermelon

½ small orange-flesh melon such as Charantais

1 small papaya

Juice of 1 lime

100g/4oz small strawberries, washed

200g/7oz tub of natural fromage frais

2 tbsp blackcurrant jam, softened

1 tbsp blackcurrant cordial or Cassis

1. Trim the pineapple and cut in half lengthwise, then cut into thin wedges and place on a platter. Cut the melons into thin wedges, remove any seeds and arrange on the platter.
2. Peel the papaya, cut in half and scoop out the seeds. Cut into wedges and place on the platter. Sprinkle the fruits with the lime juice, place the strawberries on top, then cover and chill until required.
3. For the dip, mix the fromage frais and jam together and swirl in the blackcurrant cordial or Cassis.
4. Serve the platter of fruits with the dip, with extra lime wedges for squeezing over.

BLUEBERRY AND BANANA MUFFINS

Children love muffins. They are a delicious treat and can be easily prepared with a little help from Mum or Dad.

Makes: 10

Preparation time: 10 minutes

Cooking time: 30 minutes

225g/8oz plain flour
2 tsp baking powder
Pinch of salt
100g/4oz light brown sugar
100g/4oz blueberries, thawed if frozen
1 tsp vanilla essence
1 medium egg, beaten
150 ml/¼ pt milk
50g/2oz butter, melted
1 large banana, peeled and mashed

Preheat the oven to 200°C/400°F/Gas 6

1. Place 10 paper muffin cases in a muffin tin – the depth needs to be at least 4 cm/1½in. In a mixing bowl, sift the flour, baking powder and salt and mix in the sugar and blueberries.
2. In a jug, mix together the remaining ingredients and then pour over the dry ingredients. Mix to form a rough batter, but take care not to over-beat the mixture.
3. Pile the batter into the muffin cases. Smooth the tops slightly and bake in the oven for 30 minutes, until risen and golden. Transfer to a wire rack to cool. Best served warm.

SALMON KEDGEREE

This traditional breakfast dish can be eaten at any time of day and is easily adapted for a buffet or brunch menu.

Serves: 4

Preparation time: 25 minutes
Cooking time: approx. 35 minutes

25g/1oz butter
1 tbsp vegetable oil
1 large onion, peeled and finely chopped
225g/8oz mixed white and wild rices
Salt and freshly ground black pepper
2 tsp mild curry powder
450g/1lb salmon fillet
4 medium eggs
3 tbsp freshly chopped parsley
3 tbsp freshly chopped coriander
150 ml/¼ pt low-fat natural yogurt
100g/4oz cucumber, finely chopped

1. Melt the butter with the oil in a large saucepan and gently fry the onion for 5 minutes until softened but not browned. Add the rices and cook, stirring, for 1 minute until well coated with the onion.

2. Pour in 750 ml/1¼pt water, season and add the curry powder. Bring to a boil, cover and simmer for about 20 – 25 minutes until tender and the water has been absorbed.

3. Meanwhile, preheat the grill to a medium/hot setting. Wash and pat dry the salmon fillets. Season on both sides and place on a grill rack. Cook for 5 – 6 minutes on each side until cooked through. Flake away from the skin into bite-sized pieces and keep warm.

4. Place the eggs in a small saucepan. Cover with water and boil for 7 minutes. Drain and rinse in cold water. Peel and quarter.

5. To assemble the dish, drain the rice if necessary and return to the saucepan. Gently fold in the salmon, eggs and 2 tbsp each of the herbs. Season well and pile on to a serving platter. Mix the yogurt, cucumber, remaining herbs and seasoning together and serve with the kedgeree.

HISTORY OF KEDGEREE

Kedgeree is a wonderful example of how the British adapted food from one part of their empire to another. *Khichri* was a hot and spicy Indian dish which combined dhal and rice and was flavoured with several spices including chilli. By the 18th century *Khichri* was accepted as a breakfast dish but with flaked fish instead of the dhal. Later the spices were modified and hard-boiled egg was added.

Placed on the side table in a silver serving dish, no Victorian or Edwardian country house was without it. There are many variations of the recipe: Mrs Beeton added a teaspoon of mustard and two soft-boiled eggs; others suggest cream to keep it moist, and cayenne pepper and saffron are sometimes added to give some heat and colour.

It is now a popular supper dish, and is less commonly served as a breakfast dish.

EGGS FLORENTINE-STYLE

A particular favourite of the Princess's, served either on a bed of spinach or encased in a jacket potato. Perfect for a television dinner, a light lunch or supper.

Serves: 4

Preparation time: 15 minutes

Cooking time: approx. 10 minutes

> 2 tsp white wine vinegar
> 4 medium eggs
> 50g/2oz butter
> 450g/1lb baby spinach leaves, trimmed
> Salt and freshly ground black pepper
> ½ tsp ground nutmeg
> 4 tbsp sour cream
> 4 tbsp grated Parmesan cheese
> 4 plum tomatoes, peeled, seeded and diced

1. Half fill a frying pan with water and add the vinegar. Bring the water to a boil, reduce to a simmer and break the eggs into the pan, keeping them apart. Cook gently for about 5 minutes until just set, or cooked to your liking. Remove from the pan using a draining spoon and keep warm.

2. Meanwhile, melt the butter in a large frying pan or wok and stir-fry the spinach for 2 – 3 minutes until just wilted. Remove from the heat, season and add the nutmeg. Drain to remove excess liquid.

3. Preheat the grill to a medium/hot setting. Place the spinach in the base of a shallow heatproof dish and arrange the eggs on top. Top each egg with a spoonful of sour cream and cheese. Cook for 2 – 3 minutes until lightly golden.

4. Transfer the eggs and spinach to warmed serving plates. Season and serve with the chopped tomato spooned around.

FILLED CROISSANTS

If you don't feel like cooking, it's easy to turn a plain croissant into a sumptuous breakfast treat. You can fill croissants with anything you would usually put in a sandwich, but the warmth from the croissant transforms a simple filling into a melting, buttery sensation!

Preheat the oven to 180°C/350°F/Gas 4. Place croissants on a baking sheet and heat for 5 minutes. Serve warm with one of the following fillings:

*   Melt a 50g/2oz caramel chocolate bar over a low heat with 4 tbsp double cream until runny. Beat together 100g/4oz medium-fat soft cheese with the same amount of fromage frais and then spoon into four split croissants. Top each with a few slices of banana and then drizzle with the chocolate caramel.

*   Whisk 300ml/½pt whipping cream until peaking and then sweeten with 2 tbsp softened strawberry jam and add a little vanilla essence. Fold in 100g/4oz chopped strawberries and divide between four split croissants. For a less calorific version you can replace the cream with yoghurt or fromage frais.

*   Fill each croissant with a few leaves of rocket (Arugula), 2 slices of Parma ham and 4 slices of fresh mango. Sprinkle each with a few shavings of Parmesan cheese and top each with 1 tbsp mango chutney.

MAUNDY THURSDAY

On Maundy Thursday the Queen performs a ceremony which can be traced back to Christ's action at the Last Supper when he washed the feet of his disciples (John 14, 5) telling them 'A new commandment I give unto you, That ye love one another.' The Latin word for command is *mandatum*, hence the name Maundy.

The custom of washing the feet took place in the monasteries when the abbot washed the feet of the monks. It was also the regular practice for the feet of the monarch to be washed at the Royal Court.

Today the Queen distributes Maundy money to an equal number of men and women appropriate to her age. Each person is presented with a purse containing Maundy Money. These have a monetary value in pence – one, two, three or four pence pieces totalling the age of the sovereign. The coins are legal tender, but the majority are kept as treasured possessions. If they are sold, their antiquarian value far outweighs the monetary one.

The ceremony had always been held in Westminster Abbey, but in 1953 this was closed for the Coronation so the ceremony was transferred elsewhere. From that time, Westminster Abbey has alternated as a venue with another cathedral. The Queen and the clergy carry posies, a reminder that they were once carried in the belief that they would ward off the plague. The clergy wear white garments and carry a towel over one shoulder, the last reminder that the ceremony's origins lie in washing the feet.

EASTER

Easter is the most important of all the Christian festivals. Who would have thought that the death of a carpenter's son from Galilee nearly two thousand years ago would have had such a profound influence on mankind, and today we are still celebrating his life which for many unites the world.

When we think of the Last Supper, we are reminded of a celebration around one table, where Christ's most trusted friends gathered to share a meal together. So whether your celebrations this Easter are a formal lunch, a special tea or a casual buffet, your dining table will be the central element for your meal and gifts.

Cover your table with a white linen or embroidered cloth, over which you could spread a smaller lace or crocheted 'runner' down the centre of the table. Make a centrepiece of spring flowers either in a planted display or as a fresh arrangement of cut flowers.

For many, the main gift at this time of year is an egg. It symbolizes a new life and is a sign of a new beginning, as winter is over and spring flowers bloom.

In China, an egg was given as a temple offering after the birth of a child; in ancient Greece and Rome, it was placed in tombs with the dead to indicate the continuance of life after death. As such, it was adopted by Christianity as a symbol of the resurrection of Christ.

Painted eggs have been traditional gifts for many years all over the world – red eggs were thought to be particularly auspicious as they depicted fire and an increasingly powerful sun. Christianity accepted eggs of this colour as representing the blood shed by Christ on the cross. Coloured eggs were known as *pace* eggs. In 1290 the household accounts for Edward I record a request for 450 to be coloured and given at Easter.

In Victorian England, hard-boiled eggs were painted and rolled down the hills in country villages to symbolize the stone which was rolled away from Christ's tomb.

The first chocolate eggs seem to have been made in France, and the custom first came to England in the 19th century, when the Victorians decorated eggs with velvets and satins at Easter. The British chocolate makers, Frys, produced their first chocolate egg for sale in 1873, Cadbury in 1875, and Rowntree in 1904.

Towards the end of the 19th century, Carl Fabergé, the Russian Imperial Crown Jeweller, designed a range of elegant ornamental eggs encrusted with precious jewels. The eggs were given by members of the Imperial Family as Easter gifts. Inside the eggs were hidden surprises like delicate representations of seasonal flowers and miniature portraits of the Royal Family. Many of these eggs are housed in museums in Russia, but it is Queen Elizabeth who owns the largest private collection of Fabergé eggs in the world.

HISTORY OF WINDSOR CASTLE

This is the most impressive and historic of the three official residences of the Sovereign. It was built as a fortress as well as a home, and the foundations were established by William the Conqueror. He regularly held court in the Castle from 1070.

The Castle's dominant feature is the round tower, elliptical in shape, which was built by Edward III. The tower is in the upper quadrangle of the Castle, and is named after the king. It is said to be haunted by an unknown spirit which wanders the corridors aimlessly.

St George's Chapel occupies the largest space within the lower ward of the Castle, and this is where the Royal Family regularly worships. The Chapel was conceived in 1477 by Edward IV, and completed by Henry VIII in 1528. Many aspects of its façade reflect the Tudor influence.

This has been the traditional burial place for eleven Kings and Queens of England including Henry VIII and his third wife, Jane Seymour, King Charles I and the Queen's father, King George VI.

Queen Victoria is one of only two recent monarchs not to be buried at St George's Chapel. She was so stricken with grief after losing her beloved Albert, that she built a separate mausoleum within the grounds of Windsor, at Frogmore, where she could mourn in private, knowing that one day they would be reunited.

The castle has witnessed many historic occasions. King John left his apartments here to go to Runnymede to sign the Magna Carta and King Charles I was taken from here to London for his trial and execution in 1649.

Windsor Castle is the Queen's favourite weekend retreat. Here she can relax, walk her dogs, ride in Windsor Great Park with relative anonymity, and escape the constant burdens of state. The Castle is open to the public throughout the year unless the Royal Family are using it for official entertaining.

EASTER MORNING AT WINDSOR CASTLE

Easter day is celebrated with great reverence by the Royal Family. Holy Communion is taken within the private chapel at Windsor Castle. The Queen then joins the rest of her family for a traditional breakfast in her private dining room. The breakfast table, covered with a white linen tablecloth and a fine lace runner, is decorated with potted primulas and sweet-scented jasmine, hyacinths and narcissi. Each place setting is surrounded by small gifts such as painted eggs in brightly coloured paper bags tied with ribbons, or cardboard eggs containing little gifts and assorted chocolate eggs.

The entire family joins in the celebration around the table to enjoy a breakfast of free-range boiled and scrambled eggs, crumpets and cinnamon-spiced Hot Cross Buns.

EASTER TEA

CINNAMON-SPICED HOT CROSS BUNS

No Easter would be complete without these warm, spiced fruit buns. Traditionally they are served at breakfast time, but they are just as good at a tea time celebration as they are a true symbol of Easter.

Makes: 12
Preparation time: 25 minutes plus rising
Cooking time: approx. 20 minutes

450g/1lb strong plain flour
½ tsp salt
1 tbsp ground cinnamon
50g/2oz light brown sugar
1 sachet /2 tsp easy-blend dried yeast
100g/4oz currants
1 tsp finely grated orange rind
50g/2oz unsalted butter, melted
1 medium egg, beaten
250ml/8fl. oz hand-hot milk

FOR THE DECORATION
75g/3oz plain flour
2 tbsp vegetable oil
1 small egg, beaten
4 tbsp milk
75g/3oz caster sugar

Preheat the oven to 220°C /425°F /Gas 7

1. Sift the flour, salt and cinnamon into a bowl and stir in the light brown sugar, yeast, currants and orange rind.

2. Make a well in the centre and add the melted butter, the beaten egg and three quarters of the milk. Mix with a round-bladed knife to form a soft dough, adding more of the milk if the mixture seems too dry.

3. Turn on to a lightly floured surface and knead for about 10 minutes until smooth and elastic. Place the dough in a bowl dusted with flour, cover with oiled clear wrap and leave in a warm place until doubled in size – this will take 1 – 1½ hours.

4. Re-knead the dough for about 2 minutes and then divide into 12 equal portions. Shape each into a ball and place a little apart on a large greased baking sheet. Cover loosely with oiled clear wrap and leave in a warm place until doubled in size – about 45 minutes.

5. Meanwhile, prepare the decoration. Place the flour in a small bowl and add the oil and 4 tbsp water to form a smooth, stiff paste. Place in a small paper piping bag and snip off the end so that you have a hole about 6mm/¼in in diameter.

6. When the buns are risen, brush with beaten egg and pipe a cross on to each one. Bake for 15 – 20 minutes until golden.

7. Whilst the buns are baking, place the milk and caster sugar with 4 tbsp water in a small saucepan. Bring to a boil and cook for 2 minutes. As soon as the buns are cooked, brush the sugar glaze over each bun. Transfer the buns to a wire rack to cool.

THE WIDOW'S SON

The Widow's Son, a public house in the East End of London, is so called from the story of a widowed woman who baked a bun for her only son, a sailor expected home for Easter. He never came. Each year she added a bun to the cluster hanging from a beam in her cottage. When she died, other occupants continued the tradition. Eventually the house was demolished and a public house was built on the site. The buns are said to have been transferred and a continuation of the tradition is ensured by a clause in the lease, which states that each Good Friday a sailor must add a bun to the collection.

SIMNEL CAKE

This fresh, modern adaptation of a traditional favourite would be welcome at any Easter tea table.

Serves: 10 – 12
Preparation time: 40 minutes plus setting
Cooking time: approx. 2 hours 45 minutes

225g/8oz unsalted butter, softened
225g/8oz light brown sugar
4 medium eggs, beaten
350g/12oz self-raising flour
1 tbsp mixed spice
225g/8oz sultanas
225g/8oz currants
100g/4oz glacé cherries, chopped
100g/4oz ground almonds
Finely grated rind of 1 lemon
Finely grated rind of 1 small orange
2 tbsp milk
200g/7oz marzipan

FOR THE DECORATION
225g/8oz marzipan
4 – 6 tsp lemon juice
100g/4oz icing sugar
½ tsp finely grated lemon rind
1 small egg white, lightly beaten
approx. 1m/39.5in length wide lilac ribbon
approx. 1m/39.5in length wide pale lemon ribbon
Small sugared chocolate eggs and frosted primulas to decorate

Preheat the oven to 150°C/300°F /Gas 2. Grease and line a 20.5cm/8in round deep cake tin.

1. In a large mixing bowl, cream together the butter and sugar until pale and creamy. Gradually beat in the eggs, adding a little of the flour to prevent the mixture from separating, until well mixed.
2. Sift in the remaining flour along with the mixed spice. Add the sultanas, currants, glacé cherries, ground almonds, citrus rinds and milk. Mix until well combined.
3. Pile half the mixture into the prepared tin. Roll out the marzipan to form a 19cm/7in round, about 6mm/¼in thick, and place over the cake mixture. Press down lightly and then pile the remaining cake mixture on top.
4. Level the surface and bake in the oven for 2 hours 30 minutes to 2 hours 45 minutes until golden and firm to the touch, and a skewer inserted into the centre comes out clean. An hour into the cooking time, cover the top of the cake with a layer of foil to prevent the cake from over browning. Allow to cool in the tin, then remove and place on a wire rack.
5. To decorate, divide the marzipan into eleven portions, and form each into a ball and set aside. Sift the icing sugar into a small bowl and stir in the lemon rind and sufficient lemon juice to form a smooth, dropping icing. Using a small spoon, drizzle the top and sides of the cake with the icing and arrange the marzipan balls around the edge of the cake.
6. Lightly brush the marzipan balls with egg white and brown each ball using a cook's blowtorch. Set the cake aside for about 15 minutes to allow the icing to set.
7. Transfer to a serving plate and tie the ribbons round the cake. Decorate with chocolate eggs and frosted flowers before serving.

Cook's note: to frost the flowers, brush each petal lightly with beaten egg white and then dust with caster sugar. Shake off the excess and allow to dry for 30 minutes before serving.

If you don't have a cook's blowtorch, arrange the marzipan balls in a grill pan and cook under a preheated hot grill for a few seconds to brown. Cool slightly before using

HISTORY OF SIMNEL CAKE

This lightly spiced fruit cake with a marzipan topping derives its name from the Latin word *simnellus*, meaning a cake baked on special occasions from fine wheaten flour. It has long been associated with Easter, although its origins can be traced back to Mothering Sunday. Girls from poor families were often sent to serve in the large wealthy households as maids or seamstresses. Their employers allowed them to bake a cake to take home to their mothers on Mothering Sunday, decorated with twelve marzipan balls to represent Christ's apostles. In most cases, however, only eleven balls feature: Judas Iscariot was not thought to deserve a place on such a cake.

MOTHERING SUNDAY

The fourth Sunday in Lent is said to have derived its name from the practice of visiting cathedrals or other 'mother' churches on this day or, more likely, from its proximity to 25 March or Lady Day, the day commemorating the Mother of God. On this day children who were living away from home would go back to visit their family.

The custom we now associate with Mother's Day evolved from an intertwining of the original custom and an American celebration. In 1907, Anna Jarvis of Philadelphia created an anniversary to commemorate the death of her mother, which had taken place on the second Sunday in May. It is said that the GIs who came over to Britain in their thousands during the Second World War were homesick for 'Mom' and so brought their custom with them.

If this is true, the May date was abandoned, and the British custom, commercialized as it has become, continues to be associated with the religious mid-Lent date.

JAM PENNIES

A simple, fun idea for Easter tea. These bite-sized jam sandwiches have been served at teatime in the Royal Household for generations, and are especially popular in the nursery.

Serves: 6

Preparation time: 10 minutes
No cooking

> 12 slices white or brown bread, cut thinly from a large square sandwich loaf
> 50g/2oz butter, softened
> 175g/6oz strawberry jam, sieved

1. Cut off the crusts from the bread, then lightly spread each slice with butter. Spread six slices with jam, and then sandwich together with remaining buttered bread. Press down lightly to seal.
2. Using a 5cm/2in plain round pastry cutter, stamp out 4 circles from each sandwich – the trimmings can be used in bread and butter pudding. Arrange on serving plate and serve as soon as possible to enjoy their freshness.

In 1982, Britain's largest-ever chocolate egg was made – it weighed 7,561lbs and was 10 feet high.

CUCUMBER SANDWICHES

No English tea would be complete without these fresh-tasting sandwiches.

Serves: 6

Preparation time: 12 minutes
No cooking

> 12 slices white or brown bread, cut thinly from a large square sandwich loaf
> 50g/2oz butter, softened
> 175g/6oz cucumber, very thinly sliced
> Salt and pepper

1. Cut off the crusts from the bread, then lightly spread each slice with butter. Arrange six slices with a few pieces of cucumber, and season.
2. Sandwich together with remaining buttered bread and press down lightly to seal. Cut into 4 squares and then slice off the corners from each to make a slightly octagonal shape. Place on a serving plate and serve as soon as possible to enjoy their freshness.

Tradition has it that if Hot Cross Buns were given to sailors, they would keep them safe from shipwreck (which may stem from the story on page 44). If kept in a house they would preserve it from fire – no small wonder as houses used to be made from timber, wattle and daub.

MINI SCOTCH EGGS

Makes: 12

Preparation time: 25 minutes plus cooling
Cooking time: approx. 10 minutes

1 dozen quails eggs
225g/8oz good quality sausage meat
2 tsp Worcestershire sauce
1 tbsp freshly chopped chives
1 tbsp plain flour
1 medium egg, beaten
75g/3oz dry breadcrumbs
Oil for deep frying

1. Place the eggs in a saucepan, cover with water, bring to a boil and cook for 3 minutes. Drain well and rinse under cold water to cool. Gently peel away the shell and allow to cool completely.

2. Mix the sausage meat with the Worcestershire sauce and chopped chives. Toss the eggs in the flour. Divide the sausage meat into 12 equal portions and flatten into a round big enough to hold one of the eggs – you may find it easier to handle if you flour your hands. Work the sausage meat around the eggs to cover completely. Form into a smooth round, making sure there are no cracks.

3. Brush with beaten egg and toss in the breadcrumbs. Heat the oil for deep frying to 190°C/375°F or until a cube of bread browns in 40 seconds. Fry the eggs in the oil for 4 – 5 minutes until golden and crisp. Drain and serve hot or cold.

Cook's note: as the sausage meat is raw, it is very important that the oil is the correct temperature. If it is too hot the eggs will look cooked, but the sausage meat is likely to be underdone.

SHROVE TUESDAY CREPES

Serve these thin, buttery pancakes simply with lemon juice and sugar. As a child I remember them being served with freshly squeezed orange juice, which appealed to my sweet tooth.

Makes: 15

Preparation time: 15 minutes plus standing

Cooking time: approx. 50 minutes

100g/4oz plain flour

Pinch of salt

2 medium eggs, beaten

300 ml/½ pt milk

15g/½oz butter, melted

Extra butter for frying

Wedges of lemon and caster sugar to serve

1. Sift the flour and salt into a large bowl and make a well in the centre. Add the eggs and half the milk and gradually incorporate the flour with the liquid. Whisk in the remaining milk to form a smooth batter, the consistency of thick cream. Allow to stand for 1 hour.

2. Re-whisk the batter and drizzle in the melted butter. Transfer to a pouring jug.

3. Heat a 12cm/5in crêpe pan until hot, carefully wipe with a little butter and pour in about 2 tbsp batter. Swirl it around the pan until it is spread evenly over the bottom in a thin layer.

4. Cook for 1 – 2 minutes until set, loosen the edges with a palette knife, and turn the crêpe over. Alternatively, with a flick of the wrist, toss the crêpe in the air and catch it uncooked side down. Cook for another minute.

5. Slide the crêpe on to a warm plate and repeat with remaining batter. Keep the cooked crêpes warm, stacking them between layers of greaseproof paper.

6. Serve the crêpes warm, rolled or folded with wedges of lemon to squeeze over, and sugar for dredging.

SHROVE TUESDAY

The day before the beginning of Lent, Shrove Tuesday heralds the start of a forty-day period of fasting for many Christians. It is the time for all good Christians to confess their sins. A bell, the Pancake Bell, was rung on Tuesday to remind them to come forward to be 'shriven', hence the name Shrove Tuesday.

Originally pancakes came from a combination of ingredients taken from the larder which would not be used during Lent – it would be a personal sacrifice to forgo fat, flour, milk and sugar for this time, as well as meat and eggs. The mixture was made up very quickly to form a batter that would make the last filling repast before a period of abstinence. The end of Lent is on Easter Sunday.

SPRING FAMILY LUNCH

Revive the dying tradition of a 'Sunday Roast' and enjoy this delicious menu with your family at any time of the year.

CROWN ROAST OF LAMB WITH LEEK AND ROSEMARY STUFFING AND MINT SAUCE

Roast lamb is a popular Easter meal, and one which, to many, represents Christ's innocence and sacrifice. Complemented with redcurrant jelly and homemade mint sauce and roasted with rosemary, it is a delicious favourite to enjoy.

Serves: 6
Preparation time: 25 minutes plus standing
Cooking time: approx. 1 hour 15 minutes

2 best ends of neck of lamb, prepared, or a prepared crown

FOR THE STUFFING
25g/1oz butter
1 tbsp olive oil
1 large leek, trimmed and shredded
2 tbsp freshly chopped rosemary
75g/3oz fresh white breadcrumbs
Salt and ground black pepper
1 medium egg yolk
Fresh rosemary and blanched leek strips to garnish

FOR THE MINT SAUCE
A bunch of fresh mint
150 ml/¼ pt white wine vinegar
4 tbsp caster sugar

Preheat the oven to 180° C /350° F /Gas 4

1. If you haven't got a ready-prepared crown, fold each prepared rack into a semicircle with the bones curving outwards. Press the two racks together and sew up each side using a trussing needle and fine string. Stand in a shallow roasting tin and push into a round crown shape.

2. Now make the stuffing. Melt the butter with the oil in a frying pan and gently fry the leek, stirring, for 3 – 4 minutes until just softened. Place all the stuffing ingredients, except the garnish, in a bowl and mix in the cooked leeks. Stir to form a firm stuffing mixture and then pile in the centre of the crown. Pack down well, and cover the stuffing with foil.

3. Roast the crown for about 1 hour to 1 hour 15 minutes, removing the foil for the last 10 minutes of cooking, basting occasionally. Remove from the oven, cover completely with foil and stand for 15 minutes.

4. Meanwhile, wash and finely chop the mint. Place in a jug and add the vinegar and sugar. Stir until the sugar dissolves, and then set aside until ready to serve.

5. Drain the lamb and place on a large serving platter, and garnish with fresh rosemary. Tie leek strips around each bone if liked or cover with cutlet frills. Serve with the mint sauce and accompany with Herb Roast Potatoes (see page 53) and freshly cooked seasonal vegetables.

HERB ROAST POTATOES

Serves: 6

Preparation time: 15 minutes

Cooking time: approx. 1 hour 10 minutes

1.1 kg/2lb 4oz medium sized potatoes such
as King Edward, Maris Piper or Romano
Salt
1½ tbsp plain flour
1½ tsp dried mixed herbs
6 tbsp vegetable oil
2 tbsp freshly chopped parsley

Preheat the oven to 180° C /350° F /Gas 4

1. Peel the potatoes and cut in half. Place in a large saucepan and cover with water. Add a good pinch of salt and bring to a boil. Cook for 7 minutes. Drain well and return to the saucepan. Knock the cooked potatoes against side of the saucepan to rough up the edges.

2. Toss in the flour, dried herbs and 2 tbsp oil until well coated. Place in a shallow roasting tin and spoon over the remaining oil. Cook the potatoes alongside the lamb for the last 45 minutes of cooking time, basting occasionally.

3. Once the lamb is cooked and drained, raise the oven temperature to 220° C/425° F/Gas 7, and return the potatoes to the oven for a further 10 – 15 minutes until golden and crisp. Drain the potatoes and serve sprinkled with chopped parsley.

DEEP-FILLED APPLE PIE

This most traditional of puddings is a particular favourite of the Royal Family. The pie is packed with sliced apples and has a hint of nutmeg, cinnamon and lemon. It is always served with *Crème Anglaise* or pouring cream.

Serves: 6 – 8

Preparation time: 30 minutes plus chilling
Cooking time: approx. 50 minutes

675g/1½lb shortcrust pastry
900g/2lb cooking apples
Finely grated rind and juice of 1 large lemon
100g/4oz light brown sugar
2 tbsp plain flour
1 tsp ground cinnamon
½ tsp ground nutmeg
50g/2oz sultanas
25g/1oz butter
1 small egg white, beaten
1 tbsp caster sugar

Preheat the oven to 190° C /375° F/Gas 5

1. Roll out two thirds of the pastry on a lightly floured surface and use to line a 23cm/9in round pie dish or tin. Chill for 30 minutes.
2. Meanwhile, peel, core and slice the apples thinly. Place in a bowl and toss in the lemon juice to prevent browning. Mix the brown sugar, flour, cinnamon and nutmeg.
3. Sprinkle a little of the sugar mixture over the bottom of the pastry, and toss the remaining mixture into the apples along with the sultanas and lemon rind. Pile into the pastry case and dot with the butter.
4. Roll out the remaining pastry to fit the top of the pie. Brush the pie edge with egg white and place the pastry over the pie. Trim the edges and seal. Make a small hole in the centre for the steam to escape.
5. Roll the trimmings and cut out leaf shapes. Brush the top with egg white and arrange the leaves on top. Sprinkle with the caster sugar. Stand the dish or tin on a hot baking sheet and bake for 45 – 50 minutes until the fruit is tender and the top is golden brown.

Cook's note: heat a baking sheet for 5 minutes before baking the pie. This helps the pastry underneath to cook better.

CREME ANGLAISE

Makes: approx. 750 ml/1¼ pt

Preparation time: 10 minutes
Cooking time: approx. 12 minutes

7 medium egg yolks
75g/3oz caster sugar
600 ml/1 pt milk
1 vanilla pod, split

1. In a large bowl, whisk the egg yolks and sugar until thick and creamy.
2. Pour the milk into a saucepan and add the vanilla pod. Heat until near boiling, then remove from the heat and pour over the egg mixture, whisking continuously.
3. Pour back into the saucepan, set over a low heat and cook, stirring, until the custard thickens sufficiently to coat the back of the spoon. Do not allow to boil. Pass through a sieve into a serving jug, and serve hot or cold.

KENSINGTON PALACE

From the reign of William III in 1689, Kensington Palace has been a Royal residence. Queen Victoria was born there, and lived there until she succeeded the throne. Queen Mary was also born there.

It became the residence of the Princess of Wales. Here she was able to enjoy the solitude and quietness of her own private walled garden, only a few feet away from her apartment within the Palace. The high red-brick walls covered with roses, wisteria and clematis offered her sanctuary during the summer months. She would regularly pick scented English roses, her favourite, from the garden and place them on her desk or by her bedside. Today, Princess Margaret, Princess Alice, the Duke and Duchess of Gloucester, the Duke and Duchess of Kent and Prince and Princess Michael of Kent all reside and retain offices in the building.

Summer

SUMMER

Lazy, hot summer days are synonymous with an assorted calendar of social events such as Wimbledon, Royal Ascot, the Henley Regatta and Buckingham Palace Garden Parties. It is the most avidly awaited season and provides us all with endless days and nights of outdoor freedom. Long, cool drinks in the garden often lead to barbecues, informal and impromptu social gatherings.

Trooping the Colour, the Queen's official birthday parade, heralds the beginning of the Royal summer season. It is followed by the Garter Ceremony at St George's Chapel, Windsor, and the four-day race calendar at Royal Ascot. I vividly remember sitting behind the Queen in her carriage, riding down the 'home straight' of the racecourse. For the first part of the journey, all around was silent, but as the crowds drew nearer, the applause and cheering grew louder and louder. As we turned into the paddock the Royal procession was greeted by a full rendition of the National Anthem, played by the brass band of the Household Division. I was always proud to witness, at such close quarters, the public display of adoration for the Queen.

In between the races and visits to the paddock, Her Majesty and her guests would take tea in the Royal Box. They would be offered an assortment of homemade ice creams, seasonal fruits, sandwiches and cakes. Champagne, Pimm's and traditional blends of freshly brewed teas would also be served.

Rows of regimentally parked chauffeur-driven limousines would dispense wicker picnic baskets crammed with edible delights. This is the ultimate in style, but unfortunately we cannot all aspire to such luxury. However, everyone can enjoy a simple outdoor meal.

Most of us look forward to summer picnics, or to suppers or parties in the garden. In the coming pages I've given you a few ideas for the social events that you might be considering, and hopefully the weather will be kind so you can enjoy yourself to the full.

A FRAGRANT SUMMER FLOWER ROSE BOWL

This beautiful fragrant summer display would enhance any dining-room table, or indeed any room for any occasion. It will bring the pastel shades and delicate perfumes of the season from the garden into your home. It may also inspire you with ideas for floral wedding displays and bouquets. This particular display incorporates the Princess's favourite flowers. I have illustrated a particularly lavish display, but the quantities given below can be adapted to create a smaller rose bowl.

Step 1

1 brick of Oasis/floral foam
A silver or glass rose bowl or other deep container
A reel of Oasis/floral foam tape
Approx. 50cm/20in floral mesh
A few sprays of greenery such as eucalyptus
About 19 large English roses
2 bunches of white stocks
About 9 pale pink peonies
About 27 stems of pink sweet peas
2 bunches of alchemilla

Step 2

Soak the Oasis or floral foam in cold water, flat side down, for at least half an hour to absorb the maximum amount of water. Trim the Oasis using a large kitchen knife to fit the size of your container. Secure in place using Oasis tape and bend the floral mesh over the rose bowl.

1.

Step 3

To arrange the greenery, begin by trimming it into short lengths, then push each length through the wire into the Oasis until it is secure. Fill out the whole container with plenty of greenery, keeping the balance on all sides to give an even, well-rounded framework for your flowers.

Step 4

Distribute the flowers throughout the greenery, making sure that you maintain an even-sided, full arrangement and a well-shaped top to the display. Finally place small sprays of the alchemilla around the other flowers to help 'soften' the arrangement.

Step 5

To finish the display, top up the container with water to prevent the Oasis from drying out, and spray the flowers with cold water using a fine plant mister to keep them fresh.

 2.

5.

3.

 4.

A BUG'S PARTY

I have chosen to illustrate this party theme as it translates well for both boys and girls.

Ugly bugs, spiders and creepy-crawlies for the boys, and pretty butterflies and ladybirds for

the girls. It is important to make the food look colourful, attractive and exciting. Bite-sized

nibbles are always the most popular, and remember to serve the savoury dishes first as

most kids have a very sweet tooth! Also, do remember to avoid foods which have strong

flavours. The centrepiece of the table is always the cake, and here I have chosen a ladybird.

If possible, turn off the lights in the room when the cake is about to

be presented – the candlelight will give a magical glow. And don't forget to tell the child

to make a wish as they blow out the candles.

GARDEN SNAILS

Makes: 12
Preparation time: approx. 20 minutes plus cooling
Cooking time: approx. 20 minutes

300g/10oz puff pastry (thawed if bought frozen)
3 tbsp tomato ketchup
100g/4oz grated Cheddar cheese
1 medium egg, beaten
A few fresh chives
A few currants, cut into small pieces
A little cheese spread
Lettuce and edible flowers to serve

Preheat the oven to 200° C/400° F/Gas 6.

1. Roll out the pastry on a lightly floured surface to a 30cm/12in square. Trim the edges to neaten.

2. Spread the ketchup over the square leaving the top 5cm/2in free of filling, then sprinkle grated cheese over the ketchup. Starting at the bottom, roll up the pastry tightly like a Swiss roll, leaving the plain pastry unrolled. Brush the top edge with water and fold over 1cm/½in twice – this will be the snail's head.

3. Cut into 12 equal portions and transfer to a baking sheet, sitting them upright. Brush with beaten egg and bake for about 20 minutes until lightly puffed and golden. Leave to cool.

4. Push 2 chives either side of the snail's head to resemble antennae. Spread currant pieces with a little knob of cheese spread and secure to the side of the snail's head to resemble eyes. Arrange the lettuce on a serving plate with the flowers and sit the snails on top to serve.

BUG AND BUTTERFLY SANDWICHES

Makes: 8

Preparation time: 30 minutes

No cooking

24 slices white bread from a ready-sliced loaf

300g tub cheese spread

12 slices lean ham

42 Twiglets or potato chipsticks

14 small cherry tomatoes

2 pitted black olives, cut into rings

4 radishes, trimmed

1 small carrot, peeled and cut into 6 sticks

½ mini cucumber, thinly sliced

A few chives

1. Cut off the crusts from the bread and, reserving about 2 tsp cheese spread, cover each slice with the remainder. Lay slices of ham over 12 slices and then sandwich together.

2. To make the Ugly Bugs, stamp out a 10cm/4in round from 6 of the sandwiches using a pastry cutter. Press 6 Twiglets or chipsticks round the sides of the circles to look like legs. Break the other Twiglets or chipsticks in half and set aside.

3. Spread a little of the reserved cheese spread on the bottom of 12 cherry tomatoes and press on to the bread in pairs to resemble eyes. Top with a small amount of the remaining cheese spread and sit a piece of olive on top. Use the broken Twiglets or chipsticks as antennae. Quarter the remaining tomatoes and arrange as mouths on the bugs.

4. For the butterflies, stamp out a butterfly shape from each of the remaining sandwiches and arrange the sliced vegetables on top to make the patterns of butterfly wings. Arrange 2 chives on each as antennae.

5. Place the sandwiches on a large flat plate to serve.

Cook's note: fill the sandwiches with any filling you like and butter the bread first if preferred. For a sweet version, fill with chocolate spread and decorate with sweets and mini marshmallows. Cover with clear wrap to prevent the sandwiches from drying before serving.

SPIDER AND
BUTTERFLY CUPCAKES

Makes: 12

Preparation time: 35 minutes plus cooling

Cooking time: approx. 20 minutes

100g/4oz caster sugar

100g/4oz butter or margarine, softened

2 medium eggs, beaten

100g/4oz self-raising flour

1 tbsp cocoa powder

A few drops strawberry essence

A few drops pink food colouring

TO DECORATE

3 liquorice Catherine wheels (or suitable length of thin liquorice)

75g/3oz ready-made buttercream

12 chocolate buttons

24 plain chocolate polka dots

Assorted tubes of writing icing

1 strawberry lance (or strawberry liquorice)

2 tbsp Hundreds and Thousands or multicoloured sugar strands

Preheat the oven to 190° C/375° F/Gas 5. Lightly grease and flour 12 buns tins.

1. In a mixing bowl beat together the sugar and butter or margarine until creamy and pale. Gradually beat in the eggs with a little of the flour. Sift the remaining flour into the mixture and fold in using a metal spoon.

2. Transfer half the mixture to a small bowl. Sift the cocoa into one bowl and add the essence and colouring to the other. Stir both mixtures. Spoon the chocolate mixture into 6 tins and the pink mixture into the other 6. Smooth over the tops and bake for 15 – 20 minutes until risen and firm. Remove from the tins and cool on a wire rack.

3. For the spiders, unreel the liquorice and cut into 5cm/2in lengths and set aside 2 pieces for the butterflies. Push 8 pieces into the sides of each of the chocolate cakes. Secure a pair of chocolate buttons on the top of each with a little icing, secure a polka dot on each and dot the middle to resemble eyes. Pipe a smiling mouth on to each.

4. For the butterflies, slice off the top layer of the pink cakes and split in half – these will be the wings. Lightly spread the tops of the cakes

with a little icing and lightly coat each wing with some icing. Push a pair of wings on to each cake and sprinkle with a few sugar strands. Cut the strawberry lance into short lengths and lay across the wings for a body. Cut the reserved liquorice into very thin strips and arrange 2 pieces per cake to resemble antennae. Detail the eyes with black writing icing and place 2 of the Hundreds and Thousands on as eyes.

5. Arrange the cakes on a flat plate to serve.

LADYBIRD MERINGUE
TOADSTOOLS

Makes: 12

Preparation time: 30 minutes plus cooling
Cooking time: approx. 45 minutes

1 large egg white
65g/2½oz caster sugar
4 tbsp ready-made buttercream
2 tsp drinking chocolate/cocoa mix
A few red Smarties or M&Ms
A tube each of white and black writing icing
100g/4oz desiccated coconut
Green food colouring

Preheat the oven to 150° C/300° F/Gas 2

1. Whisk the egg white until very stiff and whisk in half the sugar until stiff and glossy. Using a large metal spoon, fold in the remaining sugar.

2. Place the meringue mixture in a large piping bag fitted with a plain 1cm/½in nozzle and pipe 12 x 4 cm/1½in rounds on to a baking sheet lined with baking parchment – these will be the toadstool tops. On another lined sheet, pipe 12 x 4cm/1½in 'stalks'. Bake for 35 – 45 minutes or until lightly browned. Leave to cool on the baking sheets and then peel them off the paper.

3. Carefully secure the stalks to the tops with the buttercream. Dust the tops lightly with the drinking chocolate or cocoa mix and secure a red Smartie on each. Decorate each by piping a head, spots and eyes on to each.

4. Secure each meringue to a serving plate with buttercream. Place the coconut in a bowl and colour with green food colouring. Sprinkle the coconut around the base of each mushroom. Make some more Smartie or M&M ladybirds to decorate the plate.

Cook's note: take care when attaching the stalks to the tops – you may find it easier if you make a small indent in the meringue for the stalks to sit on. You may need to trim the ends of the stalks in order to make them stand up in the buttercream. Alternatively, you can simply arrange the mushrooms on a serving plate on their sides.

SPIDER'S WEB COOKIES

Makes: 12

Preparation time: 30 minutes plus cooling and setting

Cooking time: approx. 20 minutes

300g/10oz plain flour
175g/6oz butter or margarine
50g/2oz ground almonds
75g/3oz caster sugar
1 medium egg, beaten
Assorted tubes of coloured writing icing
12 brown Smarties or chocolate buttons
24 chocolate polka dots

Preheat the oven to 180° C/350° F/Gas 4

1. Sieve the flour into a bowl then rub in the butter or margarine until the mixture resembles fresh breadcrumbs. Stir in the ground almonds, sugar, beaten egg and enough water to form a firm dough.

2. Knead on a lightly floured surface until smooth, then roll out to a thickness of 6mm/¼in. Using a 7.5 cm/3½in round cutter, stamp out 12 circles, rerolling as necessary. Place on lightly greased baking sheets and chill for 30 minutes, then bake for 15 – 20 minutes until firm and lightly golden. Cool for 10 minutes, then transfer to a wire rack to cool completely.

3. To decorate, pipe a web design on to each biscuit. Place a chocolate button in the centre of each web – this will be the spider's body – and secure 2 polka dots on top with icing. Pipe detail on to each polka dot to resemble an eye. Pipe 8 legs on to each spider and stand for 10 minutes to set before serving.

CREEPY-CRAWLIES
IN JELLIES

Makes: 12

Preparation time: 20 minutes plus cooling and setting

No cooking

2 packets green jelly/gelatin

2 packets yellow jelly/gelatin

350g/12oz assorted jelly (gummy) bug sweets –
    not sugar-coated

2 packets orange jelly/gelatin

1. Make up the green jelly according to the packet instructions. Cool
   and then pour into 12 small plastic cups or dishes. Chill until set.

2. Make up the yellow jelly according to the packet instructions and
   allow to cool. Sprinkle a few jelly bugs on to each of the green
   jellies and then pour the liquid yellow jelly on top. Chill until set.

3. Make up the orange jelly according to the packet instructions and
   allow to cool. Pour over each jelly and chill until set.

4. Decorate the jellies with more jelly bugs, snakes and lollipops as
   required.

LADYBIRD BIRTHDAY CAKE

Cuts into approx. 32 slices

Preparation time: 2 hours plus cooling and drying

Cooking time: approx. 40 minutes

450g/1lb caster sugar

450g/1lb butter or margarine, softened

8 medium eggs, beaten

450g/1lb self-raising flour

1 tsp vanilla essence

500g/1lb 4oz ready-made buttercream

4 tbsp strawberry jam, softened

300g/10oz black-coloured fondant icing

225g/8oz red-coloured fondant icing

50g/2oz white fondant icing

2 black pipe cleaners

250g/9oz desiccated coconut

Green food colouring

Silk flowers and sweets to decorate

Preheat the oven to 190° C/375° F/Gas 5. Grease and flour 2 x 23 x 28cm/9 x 11in oblong cake tins or clean roasting tins.

STRAWBERRY SLUSH

A delicious and nutritious drink, full of vitamin C.

Serves 4

No cooking

12 water ice cubes

12 lemonade ice cubes

30 strawberries

cup of water

1. Blend ice cubes until crushed.
2. Add strawberries and blend until thick and smooth, adding a cup of water if necessary.
3. Serve in tall glasses with bendy straws.

---

1. In a large bowl, beat together the sugar and butter or margarine until pale and creamy. Gradually beat in the eggs with a little of the flour.

2. Sieve the rest of the flour into the bowl and add the vanilla essence. Fold in using a large metal spoon. Transfer to prepared tins, smooth the surface and bake for 35 – 40 minutes until golden, risen and firm to the touch. Loosen from the tins, but do not remove. Stand on wire racks to cool, then turn on to a board, one on top of the other.

3. Cut round the cakes to form into an egg shape – this will be the main body of the ladybird (keep the trimmings and use them for trifles or cake crumbs for truffles). Separate the cakes and spread one half with 225g/8oz buttercream and then the jam. Sandwich the halves back together and press down gently.

4. Using a large sharp knife, carefully 'shave' the top cake to round off the body and slightly narrow off the head end. Soften the remaining buttercream and spread all over the cake to cover it evenly.

5. Roll out the black fondant on a surface lightly dusted with icing sugar and use to cover one third of the narrowest part of the cake. Trim, neaten and reserve the trimmings.

6. Roll out the red fondant as above and cover the rest of the cake, overlapping the red on top of the black. Trim, neaten and reserve the trimmings.

7. Score down the middle of the red fondant to resemble wings. Score the black fondant to separate the head from the body.

8. Roll out the black fondant trimmings and stamp out 8 small circles. Secure 6 to the red body with a little water to resemble the ladybird's spots. Roll out the white fondant and stamp out 2 small circles. Secure to the head with water, and secure the remaining 2 black circles on top to look like eyes. Cut out small crescent-moon shapes from the white fondant and secure to the eyes to resemble highlights. Cut a small red mouth from the red fondant trimmings and secure to the cake.

9. Press pipe cleaners into the ladybird's head for antennae and mould 2 small black balls of fondant on to the ends. Allow the cake to stand for at least 2 hours, preferably overnight, lightly covered with clear wrap or greaseproof paper, so that the fondant will dry out.

10. To serve, place the coconut in a bowl and toss in a few drops green food colouring. Mix well. Sprinkle over a cake board and place the ladybird cake on top. Decorate with silk flowers and sweets before serving.

CHILDREN'S PARTIES

Everyone remembers attending a party when they were young. It is usually the first social event we encounter and they can form some of our earliest memories. With a little imagination, a child's party can be a magical event and may provide a talking point for other children and their parents.

Children's parties must be well planned so you should make a timetable for the day and try to stick to it, and be prepared for any eventuality! Young children tire quickly, so a two-hour party is probably about the right length. They also need constant supervision and attention, so you should recruit some willing helpers to assist you.

A themed party is a good idea. Choose something based on a personal hobby or interest – outer space, dinosaurs, monsters, modes of transport, animals, fairies and pixies, teddy bears are all successful themes and, above all, the party must be fun, colourful and exciting.

Choose the venue carefully. Outdoor parties are much easier to control, as you don't have to worry so much about spillages and mess, but you do need a contingency plan in case of bad weather. Decide how many children to invite. Ask yourself how many parties your child has been invited to during the past year. Those children should be invited back as a matter of principle, regardless of how many times you have seen them since. Ask the birthday child who they would like to be invited as well.

Now you are ready to send out the invitations. These could be designed to match the party theme. Don't forget to include the date, venue, party theme and the start and finish time. Try to send them out about two weeks in advance and indicate that a reply would be helpful, giving your name and telephone number.

On the day of the party, make the table look as bright and inviting as possible. Coloured disposable tablecloths and tableware are the order of the day, and balloons, paper napkins, streamers, paper hats and bendy straws will provide a splash of colour.

You could tie a helium-filled balloon to the back of each child's chair, and afterwards they can take them home. You will also need a portable music player on hand for the games, and a camera to capture all those wonderful moments.

Having witnessed many children's parties, I can tell you that the following running order is the best and has been tried and tested many times! For children arriving at the party, it is customary for them to bring a card and small gift for the birthday child. You need to keep them occupied from the very start, so a drawing or painting table is a good idea. The best picture could win a prize. This gives you time to allow all the children to arrive before the party officially begins.

Let the children jump up and down as much as they like at the beginning of the party. Work them into near exhaustion with energetic games whilst their tummies are empty! Once the tea is over it is the time to play quieter games like the traditional English game Pass the Parcel. Place a small present or sweet in between each layer of paper, so that every child will win a prize. You might want to introduce an entertainer like a magician or clown at this stage, or play a short video to quieten them down before going home.

When the children leave the party, it is customary for them to receive a 'goody bag' which again could have the same theme as the party. It usually contains some sweets, a small toy and a piece of birthday cake. Put a little note inside to thank them for coming to the party. Prepare these bags in advance and label them with each child's name.

Although you'll be thoroughly exhausted, the party will have been a magical day for your child, and the photographs you took will be a happy souvenir for you and your children in the years to come.

GAMES

Games are an essential part of any party. A mixture of noisy, quiet and energetic games is the best approach. Make a list of the games you intend to play. It is always advisable to have a larger selection of games than you may require. There are many timeless classics like Pass the Parcel and Musical Chairs which can be adapted to suit your party. But here are some ideas which fit into the theme we have chosen.

LADYBIRD, LADYBIRD – each child is given a sheet of paper with a picture of the main body of a ladybird on it. They will also need a pencil or crayon and a dice. In turn, each child rolls the dice, the number on the dice corresponding with the body parts of the ladybird:

'1' = legs, of which there are 6
'2' = wings, of which there are 2
'3' = eyes (2)
'4' = antennae (2)
'5' = spots (4)
'6' = they can draw any part they need
For example, if the child rolls a '2', he or she can draw one of the ladybird's wings, and so on. The first child to complete their ladybird is the winner.

MUSICAL BUGS – place large cut-out pictures of bugs on the floor in an open space, one per child to start with. Turn the music on and let the children dance around the bugs. When the music stops they must jump on to the nearest bug. After the first interval, remove a bug, and then continue. At each interval, remove a bug and a child will be eliminated, until there is only one child left, the winner.

PIN THE SPIDER TO THE WEB – create a spider's web using lengths of string pasted on to a piece of black cardboard. Cut out one cardboard spider per child and write their name on it. Secure a piece of sticky tape to the bottom. The children then take turns being blindfolded, turned round three times and then gently guided towards the web. The child who manages to secure their spider closest to the centre of the web is the winner.

PICNIC

This is the season for entertaining al fresco and for taking picnics to the countryside or the coast.
There is something for everyone in this section of easily prepared food which will set the scene
for the perfect day out.

ITALIAN CHEESE AND SALAMI VEGETABLE PICNIC LOAF

Serves: 6

Preparation time: 30 minutes plus chilling
No cooking

1 x 400g/14oz round country-style French loaf
225g/8oz red pimento, drained and finely sliced
100g/4oz pitted black olives, drained and chopped
100g/4oz pitted green olives, drained and chopped
4 tbsp vinaigrette salad dressing
100g/4oz cold cooked green beans, cut into short lengths
1 small red onion, peeled and finely shredded
100g/4oz Italian salami, thinly sliced
175g/6oz mozzarella cheese, thinly sliced
A small bunch fresh basil leaves
Freshly ground black pepper

1. Cut the bread across the middle and scoop out the inside crumbs to make a base and lid.
2. Mix the pimento, olives and vinaigrette together and place half in the bottom of the hollowed out loaf. Top with half the beans, red onion, salami and cheese, packing down well. Sprinkle with half the basil leaves. Season with black pepper.
3. Repeat this with the other half of the ingredients, packing down well after each layer. Put the bread lid on top, wrap up tightly and chill for at least 1 hour.
4. Carefully cut into 6 wedges. Wrap in waxed paper and then brown paper. Tie with string and place in the picnic basket.

Cook's note: for a vegetarian version of this loaf, omit the salami and replace with 225g/8oz sliced artichoke hearts.

MINI CORNISH PASTIES

Makes: 12

Preparation time: 30 minutes

Cooking time: approx. 25 minutes

100g/4oz potato, peeled and finely diced

100g/4oz carrot, peeled and finely diced

1 small onion, peeled and finely diced

225g/8oz lean beef steak, trimmed and finely diced

Salt and freshly ground black pepper

450g/1lb shortcrust pastry

1 medium egg, beaten

Preheat the oven to 220° C/425° F/Gas 7

1. In a mixing bowl, combine the potato, carrot, onion and beef and season well.

2. Roll out the pastry thinly on a lightly floured surface. Using a 10cm/4in round cutter stamp out 12 rounds, re-rolling as necessary. Divide the mixture between each round, and brush the edges with egg.

3. Bring up the edges of each pasty to meet on top. Crimp the edges together by pinching gently with the finger and thumb to seal.

4. Place on a baking sheet and brush with beaten egg. Bake for 10 minutes then lower the heat to 180° C/350° F/Gas 4 and cook for a further 15 minutes until golden and cooked through. Allow to cool and chill for 1 hour before packing.

Cook's note: you will need to chop the ingredients for the pasty very finely so that they fit into the pastry rounds. Alternatively, for a slightly less authentic version, grate the vegetables and mince the meat in a food processor.

HISTORY OF THE CORNISH PASTY

The pasty is an ingenious method of a British portable lunch. Traditionally the pasty is food baked in a pastry case without this being put in any container. The name pasty comes from old French *pastee* and medieval Latin *pasta* meaning dough, or as its name implies, paste. Originally it had only one ingredient, usually venison.

Cornwall is proud of its pasty; only a Cornish woman can make a good one and the saying goes that the Devil's afraid of coming to Cornwall in case he is baked in a pasty.

A true Cornish pasty is said to contain only steak, potatoes and onions, but there are variations – chicken and rabbit with onions, mutton with turnip and onion. Some pasties used to have meat and potato filling at one end and a jam or fruit filling at the other, thus providing a complete meal.

1. In a mixing bowl, cream together the butter and sugar until pale, light and creamy. Beat in the egg, buttermilk and orange rind.

2. Sift the flour and baking powder into the orange butter mixture and fold in using a large metal spoon. Pile into the prepared tin and smooth off the top. Bake in the oven for 40 – 45 minutes until golden and firm to the touch.

3. Five minutes before the end of cooking, prepare the syrup. Pare a few strips of orange rind away using a vegetable peeler and cut into short thin strips. Extract the juice from the orange. Place the sugar and orange juice and rind in a small saucepan and heat, stirring, until dissolved. Raise the heat and boil for 2 – 3 minutes until syrupy. Remove from the heat and stir in the orange flower water.

4. As soon as the cake comes out of the oven, prick all over with a cocktail stick. Spoon the syrup over the cake, rotating and tilting the cake so that the syrup is evenly distributed. Sprinkle with lavender to taste. Place on a wire rack until cold and then remove from the tin. Lay a sheet of baking parchment or greaseproof paper over the sugary top and then wrap and pack. Cut into 8 triangular portions to serve.

Cook's note: if preferred, replace the orange with lemon or lime.

ORANGE FLOWER
AND LAVENDER CAKE

Serves: 8

Preparation time: 20 minutes plus cooling
Cooking time: approx. 45 minutes

50g/2oz unsalted butter, softened
125g/4½oz caster sugar
1 medium egg
5½ tbsp buttermilk
1 tsp finely grated orange rind
150g/5oz plain flour
1 tsp baking powder

FOR THE SYRUP
1 large orange
100g/4oz caster sugar
1 tsp orange flower water
1 – 2 tsp dried lavender

Preheat the oven to 180° C/350° F/Gas 4. Grease and line an 18 cm/7in square cake tin.

CHAMPAGNE, STRAWBERRIES
AND CREAM

For the perfect summer picnic, there's nothing more delicious than a bowl of tempting strawberries, whipped cream and the fizz of dry champagne. Allow 100g/4oz small strawberries per person, and wash and dry them before packing – not too tightly otherwise they will bruise. Place 3 or 4 washed and patted dry rose-scented geranium leaves in a small bowl of white sugar, and stir 1 – 2 tbsp rosewater into 300 ml/½ pt whipped cream, to serve with them. Don't forget to chill the champagne well before packing into a bottle-shaped cool-bag.

PIMM'S

One of the most popular summer drinks is Pimm's. Usually it is made up with gin and lemonade and is served with plenty of ice, slices of cucumber, orange, apples and strawberries, with sprigs of mint and borage flowers. The Royal way to serve Pimm's is to replace the lemonade with champagne.

SUMMER ROYAL OCCASIONS

ASCOT – this takes place every June in the third week of the month at the racecourse in Surrey, and it lasts for four days. It is really a sign that summer is on its way. Men wear lounge or morning suits with a top hat – gloves aren't usually worn these days. Most ladies wear hats as well; indeed, you will not be allowed into the Royal Enclosure without one! Thursday is Gold Cup day and is also known as 'Ladies' Day', as this is *the* day, above all others, when the ladies make an effort to be the most fashionably dressed and wear their most extravagant headwear. All ticket holders and guests are checked in, and no cameras are allowed.

HENLEY REGATTA – the Henley Regatta has taken place every summer for the last 150 years. It is held in the first week of July and turns the usually quiet town of Henley-on-Thames in Oxfordshire upside down. Picnicking and watching the rowing races is free on the towpath alongside the 1½-mile course. If you want to be seen though, you should head for the

Stewards' Enclosure. In here, men wear jackets or a blazer, tie or cravat and aren't allowed to remove their jackets, no matter how hot! Ladies wear hats and long, floaty dresses – no knees are allowed to be shown, nor trousers worn! The Stewards' Car Park is *the* place to have your picnic, preferably eaten from the family silver, set out upon tables and chairs in front of your Rolls-Royce or Bentley!

WIMBLEDON – during the last week of June and first week of July, whilst the court is in residence at the Palace of Holyroodhouse in Edinburgh, the All England Lawn Tennis and Croquet Club in London's SW19 comes alive with a huge tennis tournament. The public queue for hours – even days – to get into the hallowed ground for a chance to see their favourite players. Tonnes of strawberries are served with cream, and gallons of Pimm's and champagne are drunk. In the Royal Box and Members' Enclosure, you must wear smart dress, jackets and ties. Even on very hot days, men are not allowed to remove their shirts.

An unusual perspective on the crowd outside Buckingham Palace waiting to greet Their Royal Highnesses The Prince and Princess of Wales, 21 July 1981.

BUCKINGHAM PALACE

This has been the official London residence of the sovereign since 1830 and is built on the site of Buckingham House, which was bought by George III in 1761 for Queen Charlotte. Most of the present building was constructed in 1825 by John Nash.

The original ceremonial entrance to the Palace was the arch situated at the west end of London's Oxford Street. This Marble Arch was removed from the Mall and placed in Oxford Street by Queen Victoria. The façade that stands in its place was built in 1913.

When the Queen is in residence, the Royal Standard flies from the flagstaff, and these days the Union flag flies at all other times. The Changing of the Guard takes place daily during the summer, and on every other day during the winter. The State Rooms of the Palace are open to the public during August and September when the Royal Family are in Scotland at Balmoral Castle.

The private and well-appointed gardens, including a lake complete with flamingos, are a perfect setting for the annual garden parties. Each party caters for approximately nine thousand individuals from all walks of life.

THE PALACE OF HOLYROODHOUSE

This is the official residence of the sovereign in Scotland, built on the site of a monastery which was founded in 1128. Its granite walls have witnessed dramatic plots and even murders. Mary Queen of Scots' lover, Rizzio, was dragged from his room in one of the turrets, down the spiral stone stairs and stabbed to death. A brass plaque marks the spot where he died.

The Palace was built in a square formation and has an inner courtyard of Italian design. The State Rooms are cavernous and are ideal for receptions and investitures, and have changed very little since the reign of Mary Queen of Scots.

Today, the Queen traditionally spends a week here in late June or early July, when she carries out her Scottish engagements, including an annual garden party in the Palace grounds. I would exercise Her Majesty's corgis every day in the Palace grounds which are overlooked by an escarpment of rock called Arthur's Seat. This dominates the Edinburgh skyline, and offers the most impressive views of the Palace from its summit.

A SUMMER WEDDING

On 29 June 1981, while thousands waited outside for a glimpse of the new Royal bride,

I vividly remember watching the Princess, in her taffeta and tulle wedding dress, laughing and

running the length of the principal corridor at Buckingham Palace.

Her shoes in one hand and her train rolled up under her arm. She was full of life and the

perfect picture of happiness, surrounded by Van Dycks, Canalettos and Rembrandts in the

Queen's Picture Gallery. Here was a young woman on the threshold of her life,

brimming with health and hope for the future.

Everyone loves a wedding. It can be the happiest and most enjoyable of all occasions. However it can also be the most traumatic, daunting and stressful to arrange. The vital key is to plan the event well in advance: you cannot begin planning too early! The day of your dreams will soon become reality. Setting a date, usually around a year in advance, and planning a venue for the ceremony and reception are the next steps after becoming engaged.

There are so many ways that you can celebrate your special day, from a straightforward church service or registry office ceremony to a blessing on a beach in the sun. Many hotels and public places have been granted a marriage licence now, so you could get married just about anywhere! You don't have to spend a fortune: a simple wedding and reception at home can be just as special, provided you have the space of course.

The budget for the wedding will vary according to specific requirements and personal taste. If the ceremony is in the morning, then two meals may be involved: a wedding breakfast and an evening buffet. If you opt for an afternoon wedding this might not be necessary. Traditionally the wedding costs are settled by the bride's parents, but increasingly both sets of parents and the couple themselves share the costs between them.

ENGAGEMENT ANNOUNCEMENT

It is traditional for engagements to be announced in the newspaper. If you want to do this, your announcement should be issued using the following example: 'The engagement is announced between Adam, the youngest son of Mr and Mrs James Broadwood of Chester, Cheshire, and Samantha Jane, only daughter of Mr and Mrs Alan Fisher of Telford, Shropshire.'

If your ceremony is to be held in a church, the parish priest or vicar will offer their full assistance, and will organize and explain the reading of 'The Banns' if appropriate. This is a traditional public announcement read out in churches belonging to the Church of England faith on three consecutive Sundays prior to the wedding. The banns were originally intended to inform the local community of a couple's intention to marry and give them the opportunity to object, as many families may have been related by blood. After discussions with the priest or vicar, you will have the basic skeleton of your service and you can then add hymns, readings and musical arrangements. You may want to have an 'Order of Service' printed for the ceremony; this acts as a guide for your guests and, of course, becomes a very personal souvenir of the day.

In Britain, a Registry Office is by far the most popular alternative to those who don't want a church wedding. Any Registry Office in the country has the power to marry couples over the age of eighteen. You only need give twenty-one days' notice, and ceremonies can be held between 8am and 6pm, Monday to Saturday, excluding Holy Days. Similarly, Americans can choose to be married at a civil ceremony in front of a judge. For many years it has been fashionable for couples to elope and marry at Gretna Green, in Scotland. Many couples have married there in secret, often without the approval of their families. For all Registry Office ceremonies you are required to provide two witnesses over the age of eighteen; no religious hymns or prayers are permitted, but popular songs and poems are allowed.

Many hotels, castles and country houses have been granted special licences to enable them to hold marriage ceremonies, and the same rules apply as for the Registry Office. Finally, if formality doesn't suit, there are travel companies which offer all-inclusive wedding holidays in

A ROYAL WEDDING RECEPTION

It would be wonderful to invite everyone you know to your wedding breakfast, but this is not practical for most of us. Even Royal weddings have their limitations, and the wedding of the Prince and Princess of Wales was no exception. Two nights before their wedding day, an elaborate ball was held for all the visiting Heads of State and dignitaries who could not attend the wedding breakfast. The guests included Her Serene Highness Princess Grace of Monaco and her son, Prince Albert and the Prime Minister, Margaret Thatcher, and her husband, Denis; all the crowned heads of Europe were represented, including Their Majesties the King and Queen of Greece. Such vivid memories of that evening will be with me for ever.

exotic locations, which means you can escape and get married under the laws of the host country. These organized holidays mean that your licence will be valid and recognized in the United Kingdom; if you are arranging this yourself, you will need to do some research and careful planning. St Lucia, known as the Honeymoon Island, is a very popular destination for weddings abroad.

WEDDING INVITATIONS

Wedding invitations are sent out no later than six weeks before the wedding by the bride's parents. They can be in the form of a greetings card or plain card, and are usually decorated with wedding symbols and designs. A good stationer's will be able to offer you numerous choices. Budget for one invitation per family, allowing an extra dozen or so for last minute guests and for making mistakes. As far as the wording is concerned, this is the correct format:

Mr and Mrs John Smith
request the pleasure of the company of

....

at the marriage of their daughter
Sarah Jane
with
Mr David Jones
at St David's Church, Leicester
on Saturday 14 August 1999 at 2pm

and afterwards at the Country Lane Hotel, Leicester

RSVP
10 Park Lane
Leicester LH2 1PP

Only the names written on the invitation are invited, so if you wish to invite entire families, including the

children, their names should be on the invitation as well. Separate invitations should be issued for the evening reception to every guest attending – even those who have received one for the wedding breakfast. Those guests attending the wedding breakfast shouldn't assume they are invited to the evening party unless a formal invitation has been issued. It is useful to send directions and maps for all venues, together with some details of overnight accommodation if your guests are travelling a long way.

WEDDING PRESENTS

A wedding list service is offered by department stores and other more specialist shops. The staff will help you compile a list of present suggestions tailored to your needs and requirements. Although some guests will want to give you something more personal, most will be grateful to receive a contact address and telephone number for your chosen store so that they can choose something from the list. Presents will be wrapped by the shop, labelled and delivered to the bride and groom at their contact address near to the wedding day.

PHOTOGRAPHS AND VIDEO

Everyone will want to see photographs of your wedding, so a photographic record of the most important day of your life (so far) is essential. A professional photographer is a must. Visit a variety of photographers and view their portfolios before making a decision. It might be useful to visit the church and reception venue with your photographer to decide exactly how to use the locations to their best advantage. Most priests will be happy for photography inside the church, but some consider flash lights an intrusion. This also applies to the use of video recorders. Remember the church is first and foremost a place of worship, so you must ask permission before the wedding.

TRANSPORT

It is practical to assume that the wedding party will require transportation to the ceremony and from there on to the wedding breakfast. A horse and carriage or a vintage car will provide perfect 'props' for photographic opportunities. It simply depends on your personal taste and style.

FLOWERS

An essential ingredient on your wedding day will be the flowers, from the bridal bouquet and buttonholes through to the church and wedding breakfast table displays.

The choice of flowers is largely personal, but a lot will depend on the season and the budget. The flowers will provide a beautiful element of style, colour and perfume on the day.

Have you ever wondered why a bride carries flowers? Flowers are a symbol of fertility and children. Strong-smelling herbs used to be entwined amongst the flowers as it was believed that the pungent smell of rosemary and thyme would help ward off evil spirits, bad luck and ill-health. Unless the bride is allergic to fresh flowers or wishes to keep her bouquet indefinitely, I consider it essential for her to carry fresh flowers on her wedding day. The Queen carried a traditional shower bouquet containing flowers from all regions of her Kingdom and Commonwealth on her wedding day, and the Princess of Wales carried a bouquet which contained stephanotis, roses, lilies of the valley and

sweet peas. You may want to select flowers which have a specific meaning, and I have compiled a list of common flowers and their connotations which you might find interesting (see page 82).

Before you decide on the flowers, think of the theme, style and colour of your wedding outfit. The bridesmaids may carry similar small arrangements to the bride's bouquet. Young bridesmaids may find it easier to

FLOWERS AND
THEIR MEANINGS

ACACIA secret love

APPLE BLOSSOM perfection

BLUEBELL lasting love

CHRYSANTHEMUM (RED) love

CHRYSANTHEMUM (WHITE) truth

DAFFODIL regard

DAHLIA good taste

FORGET-ME-NOT true love

GERANIUM true friendship

HOLLY enchantment

HONEYSUCKLE bonds of love

IVY fidelity

JASMINE sensuality

LILAC first emotions

LILY OF THE VALLEY happiness

MIMOSA sensitivity

ROSE love

SNOWDROP hope

STEPHANOTIS travel

STOCK lasting beauty

SUNFLOWER adoration

TULIP love

VIOLET faithfulness

WISTERIA I cling to you

carry a posy or small basket of flowers. Recently I saw a little girl carrying a 'wand' complete with a glittering star! You may also want to wear flowers in your hair, and provide headdresses for your bridesmaids.

If the men are wearing morning dress or frock coats then you will need to provide buttonholes. There is nothing more attractive or stylish than a simple rose or a few stems of lily of the valley, if in season.

At the church, the doorway can be transformed with climbing roses in baskets or pots, or topiary trees on either side of the door. One or two displays of large lilies like Longi or Casablanca look stunning at the altar. Make sure that the stamens are removed to avoid any mishaps on dresses and cassocks! The ends of pews can be decorated with simple hand-tied natural posies. If there is another wedding in the church on the same day, you will have to consult with the other families when it comes to decorating the church, and a compromise will have to be reached.

You may be advised to check the church's regulations on the scattering of petals or confetti; I have seen bridesmaids scattering rose petals from baskets all the way up the aisle, much to the disapproval of the priest.

At the wedding breakfast, you will probably want to decorate each table with a small arrangement. Candles look good, especially floating ones, if it is an evening reception. The top table can be decorated more grandly with swags of greenery draping up and around the sides of the table – ivy works particularly well for this.

Whatever your taste, the flowers you choose will add an extra special dimension to your wedding day.

THE WEDDING CAKE

The centrepiece of your wedding breakfast will be your cake. A local baker or cake specialist will make the cake to your specification. Although it is traditionally a rich fruit cake, many couples now are choosing a chocolate or plain sponge cake in preference. The caterers should provide a knife for the important ceremony of the 'cutting of the cake'. Sometimes pieces of cake are boxed and sent to those who were unable to attend, and small cake boxes are usually offered when your order your stationary. You may also like to explore the idea of 'favours'. This is an American idea of providing your guests with a small 'keepsake' by which to remember your happy day. These are usually placed on the table at the wedding breakfast. Traditionally sugared almonds are wrapped in small pieces of sheer fabric, but increasingly other gifts like small boxes of chocolates or miniature bottles of brandy or champagne are given. Another excellent idea is to give disposable cameras for your guests to take pictures of incidents that you might miss.

THE WEDDING DAY

After months of planning, the big day arrives and, although no two weddings are alike, I have compiled a running order to guide you through your big day, explaining the correct etiquette where appropriate.

The ushers, best man and groom are the first to arrive at the church, and should be in place about thirty minutes before the ceremony begins. The ushers control the flow of the congregation and are responsible for handing out the 'Order of Services' and for making sure

Special mementos from the wedding of Their Royal Highnesses the Prince and Princess of Wales.

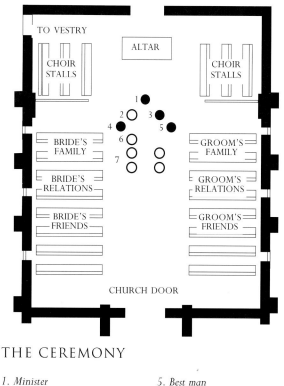

THE CEREMONY

1. Minister   *5. Best man*

2. Bride   *6. Chief bridesmaid*

3. Bridegroom   *7. Bridesmaids*

4. Bride's father

that the guests sit in their proper places. The first two rows of seating are allocated to the immediate family. Guests of the bride and the bride's family sit on the left-hand side of the church, and the groom's on the right-hand side. The best man and groom take their seats at the front right-hand side of the church. The congregation arrives about fifteen to twenty minutes before the ceremony begins. The groom's parents will then arrive and be shown to their seats, directly behind their son, by a specially designated usher. It is worth noting here that divorced parents of the bride and groom should sit together. Second husbands and wives should sit further behind with friends and the rest of the family. The bridesmaids are the next to arrive, with the bride's mother, and they wait at the entrance for the bride to arrive with her father. The bride's mother is the last to be seated, again by a designated usher, and the service is ready to begin.

As the processional music starts, the congregation stands, the groom and best man take their place at the altar steps, and the bride, with her bridesmaids and pageboys, walks down the aisle, on the left arm of her father. It is traditional for the bride to wear her veil covering her face until she reaches the altar, and then it is lifted to greet the groom. The chief bridesmaid may help with the veil and train, and will take the bridal bouquet from the bride. The bride's father joins his wife once he has 'given the bride away'.

The ceremony begins and the marriage takes place. The couple sign the register in the vestry in the presence of the best man, bridesmaids and both sets of parents to witness their signatures.

On leaving the church, the bride leaves on the arm of her husband, followed by the bridesmaids and pageboys. The chief bridesmaid is escorted by the best man, followed by the bride's mother with the groom's father, and the groom's mother escorted by the bride's father. Outside the church, photographs usually take place and then everyone departs to the reception.

The first meal after the wedding ceremony is traditionally called the wedding breakfast. The bride and groom should be the first to arrive at the venue, shortly followed by the bridesmaids, best man and both sets of parents. It may be appropriate for the immediate party

SEATING PLAN

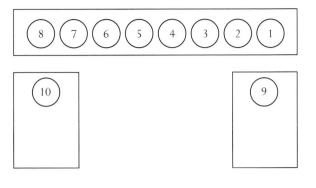

Top table

1.	Groom's mother	6.	Groom's father
2.	Bride's father	7.	Chief bridesmaid
3.	Bride	8.	Best man
4.	Bridegroom	9.	Groom's family
5.	Bride's mother	10.	Bride's family

to form a reception line as the guests enter, thus making sure everyone has an official greeting. Your guests should then be offered a drink such as champagne, buck's fizz, sherry or Pimm's, plus a non-alcoholic choice as well. After about thirty minutes, the toast master or best man asks everyone to take their seats at the tables.

Once your guests have found their seats, the toast master or best man will ask everyone to stand and welcome the bride and groom 'Mr and Mrs ....'. It is customary for the guests to clap whilst the couple take their places at the 'top table'. The meal is then served.

THE SPEECHES

These begin before the wedding cake is cut, and the first to be announced by the toast master or best man is the bride's father. His speech is often poignant and moving and will usually recall memories of his daughter's life. He also welcomes the bridegroom's parents. He then proposes a toast to the future health and happiness of the newly married couple, and everyone stands to raise their glasses, not 'clink' them together, to the bride and groom, who remain in their seats.

The groom is then asked to stand and speak on behalf of his new wife. He thanks both sets of parents, his best man and may want to remember someone dear or elderly, or an absent friend. He toasts the health of the bridesmaids and everyone stands, bar the bridesmaids. Often small gifts are given at this point as a further token of thanks. It is also at this point that the bride and groom may wish to present their mothers with a bouquet of flowers to thank them for their help and support.

Inevitably the day revolves around the bride, and although not traditional, she may like to say a few words herself. The important things to remember are to be confident, relaxed and speak slowly and clearly. This speech will surprise everyone and will be very warmly received.

The last speech comes from the best man, and is traditionally the most amusing and jovial. This is his opportunity to shine and tell some amusing stories about the groom and the bride. He speaks on behalf of the bridesmaids and thanks them for carrying out their duties. To conclude, he may read a selection of cards and telegrams from a pre-selected bundle sent by those who were unable to attend the wedding. He will propose a toast to the bride, and everyone then stands to raise their glass to her.

After the speeches, the wedding cake is cut by the bride and groom, and then the rest of the cake is cut up into smaller pieces by the caterers and distributed amongst the guests. The Royal Family usually give their guests a piece of wedding cake in a monogrammed box as a keepsake of the day.

Towards the ends of the reception, the bride may wish to toss her bouquet over her shoulder to a gathered ensemble of unmarried ladies. The one who catches the bouquet is, by tradition, the next to marry. However, some brides prefer to place their bouquet on the grave of a loved one. Royal brides always have their bouquets placed on the tomb of the Unknown Soldier in Westminster Abbey.

Catrina Skepper's exquisite wedding dress by Catherine Walker features an épaules dénudées neckline, fitted bodice, transparent fluted sleeves and low-cut back that gently cascades into a flowing skirt.

The dual train is hand-scalloped with intricate floral cording. The Lyon lace is illuminated with 44,000 pearl and crystal beads and was meticulously re-embroidered by hand with 300m of duchess satin cording to echo the elongated silhouette. (Wedding to Alessandro dei Conti Guerrini Maraldi, Brompton Oratory, Saturday 24 April 1999.)

BEST MAN

Traditionally the best friend or brother of the groom – although there is no hard and fast rule that the best man has to be male! – and has much of the responsibility regarding the groom's welfare on his shoulders. He organizes the 'stag night' – the all-male celebration of the groom's last night of bachelorhood. The bride would be well advised to persuade the best man to organize it at least a week before the wedding to give her intended enough time to recover from his ordeal.

On the wedding day, the best man is responsible for the groom. He ensures that the groom is dressed in the appropriate attire and that he and the groom have a buttonhole to wear. He is entrusted with the wedding rings and hands them to the priest or vicar during the wedding service. He pays the appropriate fees to them, and to the choir, bell ringers and church wardens for their services on the day. He advises the ushers and ensures that the event is running to time.

The best man may wish to place a bottle of champagne and two glasses in the wedding vehicle for the newlyweds' journey from the church to the reception. He arranges all other aspects of transport for the rest of the bridal party as well. If there is honeymoon luggage, he makes sure that it goes to the correct venue, and that it is safely secured.

Finally, his main duty on the day is to provide an entertaining and witty speech of about five minutes in length at the reception.

CHIEF BRIDESMAID

Chosen by the bride, either a best friend or sister. If she is married, she is rather old-fashionedly called 'Matron of Honour'. Her responsibilities are to the bride what the best man's are to the groom. She organizes the 'hen night' – a celebration amongst female friends. She checks the bridal flowers and corsages and will assist the bride and any other bridesmaids to dress.

She travels with the other bridesmaids alongside the bride's mother to the church. The bride's dress, train and veil may need attention before the walk down the aisle and

she should see to this. At the altar, the bride passes her bouquet to the chief bridesmaid. This is then handed back later on, ready for the signing of the register.

If there is a change of clothing or honeymoon luggage to coordinate, she should organize this in conjunction with the best man.

USHERS

Chosen from friends and family, they are in charge of seating the families in their correct places. One is designated with the task of showing the bride's mother to her seat. They may also be in charge of the transport arrangements to and from the church, and the handing out of the service and prayer books.

When the guests arrive at the church, the ushers should ask them whether they are with the bride or groom's family, and then see them to their seats.

WEDDING SUPERSTITIONS

If you're superstitious, then these quirky pieces of information will be of interest to you:

- It is bad luck for the groom to see his bride on the morning of their wedding day, especially in her wedding dress. His first sight of her should be as she approaches the altar steps or the minister in charge of the ceremony.

- Traditionally the sign of purity, the white wedding dress was made popular by Queen Victoria when she married Prince Albert. It is said to be unlucky for anyone to wear green when attending a wedding.

- A bride should not cry on the morning of her wedding as this is bad luck. She must also leave through the door of her home, leading with the right foot to ensure good fortune.

- A black cat, rainbow, chimney sweep, toad or spider is a symbol of good luck if seen by the bride on her wedding day. If she is woken up by songbirds, then good fortune will smile on her.

- There is a saying, 'Happy is the bride whom the sun shines on', but in Germany, if rain falls on the bride, this is considered a blessing.

- Bad luck is said to prevail if a pig or funeral party crosses in front of the wedding car.

- There is an old wives' tale that says that if a bridesmaid sleeps on a piece of wedding cake, she will dream about the man she will marry. It is also said: 'Three times a bridesmaid, never a bride'.

- It is good luck for the groom to carry his new wife over the threshold of their home for the first time.

- The most famous bridal superstition is that she should wear something old, new, borrowed and blue for luck.

WEDDING ANNIVERSARIES

It is especially romantic to remember your wedding day each year by surprising each other with a gift made from the material associated with that anniversary. Here is a guide to help you with your choice:

First	Cotton
Second	Paper
Third	Leather
Fourth	Silk or Flowers
Fifth	Wood
Sixth	Sugar or Iron
Seventh	Wool or Copper
Eighth	Bronze
Ninth	Pottery
Tenth	Tin
Eleventh	Steel
Twelfth	Silk, fine linen or leather
Thirteenth	Lace
Fourteenth	Ivory
Fifteenth	Crystal
Twentieth	China
Twenty-fifth	Silver
Thirtieth	Pearl
Thirty-fifth	Coral
Fortieth	Ruby
Forty-fifth	Sapphire
Fiftieth	Gold
Fifty-fifth	Emerald
Sixtieth	Diamond
Seventieth	Platinum

The gold wedding ring symbolizes the circle of life. Royal wedding rings are traditionally made from a nugget of Welsh gold, and are fashioned by Garrard, the Crown Jeweller.

Autumn

AUTUMN

The greens of summer are replaced by the rich, dark and golden hues of autumn.

Hedgerows are laden with berries and orchards are abundant with fruit.

At the end of the social season in London, the Royal Household moves lock, stock and barrel to the Scottish Highlands and the idyllic setting of Royal Deeside. This is the Queen's private summer residence, although the affairs of State continue and Her Majesty is never 'off duty'. This is primarily a time for the Royal Family to relax and enjoy the invigorating Highland air. Wild berries grow profusely on the moors and in the hedgerows. Blackberries, blueberries and raspberries are particular favourites at breakfast and teatime, whether in a natural compote or gently stewed into a preserve. Stags are stalked to provide venison for the Royal table and the River Dee is fly fished for the world's best-known salmon.

Before the legendary Scottish mists descend and winter takes a hold, an outdoor life will have been enjoyed by everyone.

A GRAND VICTORIAN-STYLE CENTREPIECE

Although this grand centrepiece looks very complicated it really is simple to execute. The skeleton for this structure is merely two cake stands placed on top of one another and they are divided by large dinner platters or plate liners. Much of this will be unseen in the finished piece, so it really doesn't matter what you use to form the base. It is, however, better to select plates with a slight dip so that the arrangement can retain some water. The Victorians loved to mix fruit and flowers together in their arrangements in order to enhance the dining table and to reflect the grand luxury of the era.

5.

1.

2.

3.

4.

Step 1

    2 cake stands
    3 large round dinner platters or plate liners
    4 bricks of Oasis/floral foam
    1 reel of Oasis/floral foam tape
    1 thin green garden cane
    1 large pineapple
    Assorted greenery: e.g. ivy, ruscus, eucalyptus, red robin
    5 bunches of fresh lavender
    A few pieces of stub wire
    5 bunches black grapes
    Assorted white flowers: e.g. small roses, trachelium
    Assorted orange flowers: e.g. arum lilies, freesia, small roses
    11 plums
    2 stephanotis plants to circle the base of your arrangement

Step 2

Arrange the cake stands and platters on top of each other to form three tiers. Soak the Oasis bricks, flat side down, in cold water for at least half an hour to absorb the maximum amount of water. Cut into smaller blocks using a kitchen knife and secure to the platters using strips of Oasis tape.

Step 3

Break the cane in half and skewer into the pineapple. Push this into the top piece of Oasis. Break the greenery into various lengths and arrange evenly around each layer. Fill gaps with small bunches of lavender.

Step 4

Twist lengths of wire round each bunch of grapes to secure them to the Oasis, then begin pushing in stems of white flowers, followed by orange flowers. Arrange the flowers, making sure you have an even balance of colour.

Step 5

Finally skewer the plums on wires and push in and around the arrangement. Unravel the stephanotis plants and trail around the base of the decoration to form a garland.

Note: to keep the arrangement fresh, water the Oasis frequently to keep it moist and then mist the foliage with a fine water spray to prevent it from drying out.

VICTORIAN DINNER

It seems appropriate to illustrate a lavish Victorian-style dinner party in the autumn section.

This is an excellent time to utilize the rich harvest of fruit, vegetables and flowers on

a somewhat grander scale.

The Victorian dinner party was an important and well-practised ritual which reflected the rich and successful lifestyle of the opulent upper classes. Grand pieces of furniture, silver, crystal and fine porcelain were signs of a family's stature and wealth, with coats of arms and ciphers often emblazoned on glassware and china in a truly Royal style.

Presentation was the essence of a Victorian table and meal times were of huge significance to the family.

The centrepiece of any dinner party is the dining table, and for the Victorians it would have been overwhelmingly extravagant. Large baskets of fruit and flowers would have surrounded silver candelabra, and the light from the candles provided a soft, warm glow to accompany the rather theatrical setting. Today, however, it would be impractical to create an exact replica dinner party, as the endless courses of turtle soup, game, sweetbreads and sumptuous sweets would be too rich for our taste buds. But it is worth noting that from them evolved the structure of the modern day formal menu: i.e. a soup starter, followed by a fish course, then a main course and finally a sweet.

The pineapple was regarded as a welcoming symbol and that is why you see it reflected in architectural designs of the period.

SMALL FISHCAKES WITH LEMON AND SORREL SAUCE

Serves: 6

Preparation time: 40 minutes plus cooling
Cooking time: approx. 30 minutes

450g/1lb skinless firm white fish fillets, such as cod
1 carrot, peeled and roughly chopped
1 small onion, peeled and halved
1 celery stick, trimmed and roughly chopped
1 bay leaf
350g/12oz cooked and mashed boiled potatoes
3 medium eggs
4 tbsp freshly chopped parsley
2 tsp mustard powder
1 tbsp Worcestershire sauce
Salt and freshly ground black pepper
100g/4oz fresh white breadcrumbs
50g/2oz butter
6 tbsp vegetable oil

FOR THE SAUCE
225g/8oz sorrel or young spinach, stalks trimmed
50g/2oz butter
50g/2oz plain flour
Finely grated rind and juice of 1 lemon
150 ml/¼ pt double cream
2 medium egg yolks
1 tsp caster sugar, to taste
Flat-leaf parsley to garnish

1. Place the fish fillets in a large frying pan with a lid and add the carrot, onion, celery and bay leaf. Pour over sufficient water to just cover the fish, bring to a boil, cover and simmer for 10 minutes until just cooked. Allow to cool in the liquid.

2. Drain the fish, reserving the cooking liquid, and flake. Place in a bowl and add the mashed potato, one egg, the chopped parsley, mustard and Worcestershire sauce. Season and mix well.

3. Beat the remaining eggs and place on a large plate. Place the breadcrumbs on another. Divide the fish mixture into 18 small portions and form each into a small 'cake' about 5cm/2in in diameter. Gently toss each in egg and then crumbs.

4. Melt the butter with the oil in a large frying pan and gently fry the fishcakes in two batches for 2 – 3 minutes on each side until golden. Drain and keep warm.

5. For the sauce, place the sorrel or spinach in a large saucepan with 2 tbsp reserved cooking liquid. Bring to a boil, cover and simmer for 2 – 3 minutes until wilted. Drain well by pressing through a sieve, then finely chop

6. Melt the butter and stir in the flour and cook for 1 minute. Remove from the heat and gradually stir in 300 ml/½ pt reserved cooking liquid. Return to the heat and cook, stirring, until thickened. Stir in the remaining ingredients with the chopped sorrel or spinach, and season well. Heat through for 1 – 2 minutes.

7. Serve three fishcakes in a pile in a pool of sauce, garnished with parsley and accompanied with lemon wedges.

Cook's note: sorrel was a popular herb in Victorian times. The broad green leaves look like spinach and have a sharp, acidic, lemony flavour. Look out for fresh sorrel at the supermarket or greengrocer. Dried sorrel has little flavour and is a poor substitute.

ROAST BEEF AND
YORKSHIRE PUDDINGS

This is our national dish. Aberdeen Angus is the richest and most succulent of all beef and is always served in the Royal Household. Sirloin was a popular cut of beef with the Victorians.

Serves: 6

Preparation time: 20 minutes plus standing
Cooking time: approx. 1 hour 20 minutes

1.75 kg/4lb rolled sirloin of beef
1 tbsp plain flour
1 tbsp mustard powder
Salt and freshly ground black pepper
1 small onion, peeled and halved
4 bay leaves

FOR THE YORKSHIRE PUDDINGS
100g/4oz plain flour
1 medium egg, beaten
300 ml/½ pt milk

Preheat the oven to 220° C/425° F/Gas 7

1. Wash and pat dry the beef. Mix the flour, mustard powder and seasoning together and sprinkle some in the base of a roasting tin, and then rub what remains into the beef fat. Stand at room temperature for 30 minutes.

2. Place the beef in the tin, push the onion close to the beef and the bay leaves under the beef. Roast for 10 minutes per 450g/1lb for rare beef; 12 – 15 minutes per 450g/1lb for medium to well done. Baste the joint occasionally to keep it moist. Transfer to a warmed serving platter, reserving the meat juices, cover and allow to stand for 30 minutes before carving.

3. Meanwhile, make the Yorkshire puddings. Sift the flour with a pinch of salt into a bowl. Make a well in the centre, add the egg and gradually incorporate the flour with the egg. As the mixture thickens, slowly pour in the milk, stirring until the mixture forms a smooth batter. Transfer to a jug and allow to stand for 30 minutes. Then re-whisk.

4. Once the beef is cooked, spoon a little of the reserved beef cooking juices in a 12-hole patty tin and place in the oven for 2 – 3 minutes until very hot. Quickly pour in the batter and return to the oven and bake for 15 – 20 minutes until well risen and golden. Serve immediately.

5. Carve the beef and serve with Yorkshire puddings, Herb Roast Potatoes (see page 53) and other roast and steamed vegetables. Accompany with gravy, horseradish sauce and English mustard.

SIRLOIN OF BEEF
AND YORKSHIRE PUDDINGS

Mrs Beeton quotes a story about how sirloin got its name, crediting it to Charles II knighting the joint at Friday Hall, Chingford, Essex. The king returned from hunting in Epping Forest and saw meat.
'A noble joint', he said, 'By George, it shall have a title'. Then he drew his sword and tapped the meat, saying, 'Loin, we dub thee knight. Henceforth be Sir Loin.'
Mrs Beeton says that the name is probably a corruption of the French *sur* (above) and *longe* (loin) into sirloin, the upper part of the loin, and though it is a pity to spoil a good story, this is probably correct.
Yorkshire Pudding, a batter pudding created from a mixture of milk, flour and eggs, had been known in medieval times. Later it was made in a huge dish placed beneath spit-roasted meat so that the fat and juices would fall into the pudding pan and give it a unique flavour and appearance. It gets its name from its county of origin.

PEARS IN PORT WINE WITH CINNAMON ICE CREAM

The simplest but most effective of all desserts. This was one of the Princess's favourites and was often served at official dinners and lunch parties.

Serves: 6

Preparation time: 1 hour plus standing, cooling and freezing

Cooking time: approx. 55 minutes

FOR THE ICE CREAM

450 ml/¾ pt single cream

1 vanilla pod

2 cinnamon sticks

3 medium egg yolks

100g/4oz caster sugar

150 ml/¼ pt double cream

FOR THE PEARS

450 ml/¾ pt ruby port

1 strip lemon rind

1 strip orange rind

4 tbsp redcurrant jelly

2 cinnamon sticks, broken in half

6 ripe dessert pears

½ lemon

'Let the number of your guests never exceed twelve, so that the conversation might be general. Let the temperature of the dining room be about 68. Let the dishes be few in number in the first course but proportionally good. The order of the food is from the most substantial to the lightest. The order of the drinking is from the mildest to the most foamy and most perfumed. To invite a person to your house is to take charge of his happiness as long as he is beneath your roof.'

Mrs Beeton quoting 'a great gastronomist' in her

Book of Household Management, 1859 – 61

1. First make the ice cream. Pour the single cream into a saucepan. Split the vanilla pod down the middle and scrape out the seeds into the cream along with the pod. Break the cinnamon sticks into half and add to the cream. Slowly bring to a boil. Remove from the heat, cover and stand for 30 minutes.

2. Whisk the egg yolks and sugar in a large bowl until pale, thick and creamy. Reheat the cream until gently simmering and then pour over the egg mixture, stirring constantly. Strain through a sieve back into the saucepan and cook over a low heat, stirring, until the custard thickens enough to coat the back of a wooden spoon. Do not allow to boil. Pour into a heatproof bowl and allow to cool completely.

3. Whip the double cream until just peaking and then fold into the custard. Pour the mixture into a freezer container, cover and place in the coldest part of the freezer. Beat the mixture 3 – 4 times at 40-minute intervals to break up the ice crystals. Seal and freeze for a further 2 hours. Stand at room temperature for about 15 minutes before serving, to make sure it is soft enough to scoop.

4. For the pears, pour the port into a saucepan along with 150 ml/¼ pt water. Add the citrus rinds, jelly and cinnamon. Bring to a boil and cook for 1 minute until the jelly has dissolved.

5. Peel the pears, leaving the stalks intact. Slice the bottoms if necessary so that they stand up straight. Rub the cut side of the lemon over the pears to prevent them from browning.

6. Stand the pears in a saucepan – you want them to stand snugly next to each other – and pour over the hot port. Bring back to a boil, skim away any surface scum, cover and simmer for 35 – 40 minutes, spooning the cooking liquid over the pears frequently, until tender.

7. Remove the pears using a draining spoon, reserving the cooking liquid, and place the pears in a heatproof dish. Return the cooking liquid to the heat and bring to a boil. Cook for 12 – 15 minutes until well reduced and syrupy. Pour the syrup over the pears through a sieve, and allow to cool, then chill for 1 hour before serving with cinnamon ice cream. Alternatively, serve hot with the ice cream.

Cook's note: it is vital that you use fresh spices for this recipe, otherwise there will be little flavour. Cinnamon bark has a very delicate flavour that is soon lost in storage.

PUNCH JELLY

Another popular dessert with the Victorians was an extremely alcoholic jelly made of rum and brandy. It was flavoured with orange and lemon and the spices cloves, nutmeg and cinnamon. The liquid was sweetened and set with gelatin. It was often poured into small punch cups or a beautiful jelly mould and allowed to set. Only a small portion was suggested, as it really did pack a punch!

Serves: 12

Preparation time: 15 minutes plus cooling and setting

Cooking time: 20 minutes

225g/8oz caster sugar

Finely grated rind of 3 lemons

Finely grated rind of 1 orange

5 cloves

Pinch of grated nutmeg

1 cinnamon stick, broken

150 ml/¼ pt rum

150 ml/¼ pt brandy

150 ml/¼ pt fresh lemon juice

1½ tbsp powdered gelatin

1. Place the sugar in a large saucepan with 600 ml/1pt cold water. Add the lemon and orange rind and spices. Bring to a boil, stirring, until dissolved and then simmer for 15 minutes.

2. Remove from the heat and pour in the rum, brandy and lemon juice. Strain the mixture through a sieve lined with muslin into a heated bowl.

3. Dissolve the gelatin in 5 tbsp boiling water and stir into the strained liquid. Set aside to cool and then pour into a 1lt/1¾ pt jelly mould or 12 punch glasses or small dishes and chill until set. Serve decorated with slices of lemon.

CLASSIC VICTORIAN FOODS

If you want to put together your own Victorian-style menu, you might find this table of food suggestions useful for ideas:

MAIN COURSES
turtle soup, truffles, pheasant, prawns, grouse pie, lobster, ham, tongue, roast beef, fillet of veal, mutton cutlets, sweetbreads, aspic jellies. Asparagus was a popular vegetable

SWEETS
compotes of fresh and dried fruits, candied fruits, jellies, fruit tarts, bavarois, iced desserts

CHEESE
Stilton

DRINKS
barley water, hot and cold punches, fresh lemonade

HIGHLAND HIGH TEA

Tea epitomizes the British way of life. From Buckingham Palace to a terraced home in the heart of England, a cup of tea is the greatest of all British traditions. Whether the tea is loose leaf Darjeeling, Earl Grey or a simple tea bag, this revitalizing and comforting brew is served in just about every household and workplace throughout the country, and it has been a tradition for many years.

Whether enjoying tea in your home, in a country garden or at a formal occasion, it is guaranteed to provide refreshment. There is always time for a 'cuppa', and at times of crisis there is always a cup of tea on hand for comfort.

By the end of the 19th century some households, because they did not take luncheon, brought their evening meal forward to fill the gap. In the north of England this became known as 'High Tea' and it centred round the drinking of what had previously been a cup of tea or an afternoon drink. In households where dinner was served later, a light meal was introduced which was often the last meal the children would have before they went to bed. At first it was just a cup of tea and a sandwich, but gradually a wider variety of cakes and fruits were added. The emergence of tea as a social event was born, and it is often associated with gossiping women in the drawing rooms of Victorian England. In 1877 the tea gown was devised as a fashionable garment suitable for such an occasion.

Taking tea at five o'clock is still a tradition observed by the Royal Family wherever they are in residence, and the Queen delights in making her own pot of tea, in a silver teapot, of course.

'A woman is like a tea bag: only in hot water do you realize how strong she is!'

Nancy Reagan

During my career, I must have served thousands of cups of tea at receptions, meetings and garden parties and this is my tried and tested way of making the perfect cuppa. The essential element of course, is boiling water.

1. Warm the teapot with boiling water. Always take the pot to the kettle, not vice versa. After 2 – 3 minutes pour the water away.
2. Spoon one teaspoonful of tea per person plus 'one for the pot' into the teapot – this does depend on the strength of tea, size of teapot and personal taste.
3. Pour over boiling water until the pot is three quarters full. Leave to 'steep' for 2 – 3 minutes, stirring once to ensure the leaves infuse properly.
4. Strain the tea into teacups and add milk or lemon, and sugar to taste – never put the milk in the teacup first.

A tea cosy will keep the pot warm, but it will also cause the tea to 'stew'.

I have put together some suggestions which could be used for a hearty Highland tea – suitable for any 'royal' table. These days, the Queen is never in her Scottish residence from October onwards. When the first snows and heavy frosts settle on the foothills of Lochnagar, it is time to return south.

BRAMBLE JELLY

Makes: 675g/1½lb

Preparation time: 20 minutes plus draining and cooling

Cooking time: approx. 30 minutes

> 900g/2lb blackberries
> approx. 450g/1lb preserving sugar
> 2 tbsp lemon juice

Preheat the oven to 140° C/275° F/Gas 1

1. Wash the blackberries thoroughly, and hull them. Place in a large saucepan or preserving pan and pour in 150ml/¼pt cold water. Bring to a boil and simmer for 10 minutes until very soft, pressing the fruit occasionally.
2. Strain the fruit and its juices through a jelly bag or some clean muslin suspended over a clean bowl – this will take about 6 hours to allow the fruit left behind to become dry – don't be tempted to squeeze the mixture.
3. Measure the juice and pour back into the saucepan. Add 450g/1lb sugar and 2 tbsp lemon juice per 600ml/1pt blackberry juice. Stir over a low heat until the sugar is dissolved. Raise the heat and boil rapidly for about 15 minutes until setting point is reached (104° C/219° F on a sugar thermometer – see below if you don't have a thermometer). Skim off any surface scum using a flat spoon.
4. Meanwhile, prepare the jars. Wash them very well in hot water, and rinse thoroughly. Dry them, and place them in the oven on a baking sheet lined with paper.
5. Carefully pour the hot jelly mixture into the prepared jars, tapping as you pour so any air bubbles are dispersed, to within 6mm/¼ in of the top. Place waxed circles from packs of jam pot covers on the hot jelly to form a seal, and then seal completely with transparent covers or lids.
6. Allow to cool, then label and store in a cool dark place.

Cook's note: to test for setting if you don't have a sugar thermometer, spoon a little of the boiling preserve on to a cold plate. Remove the rest of the jelly from the heat. Allow the spoonful to cool and then push it with your finger. If the jelly has reached setting point the top will have set and the preserve will wrinkle when you push it. Continue boiling the jelly if necessary.

TEATIME SCONES

Traditionally served unfruited, if you omit the sugar and add a pinch of salt, these scones can be eaten with cheese. Simply twist a scone in the middle to break it open – you don't have to slice it.

Makes: 12

Preparation time: 15 minutes

Cooking time: approx. 15 minutes

> 450g/1lb self-raising flour
> 100g/4oz butter, cut into small pieces
> 100g/4oz caster sugar
> 250 ml/9 fl oz milk
> 1 small egg, beaten

Preheat the oven to 220° C/425° F/Gas 7

1. Sift the flour into a bowl. Add the butter and rub into the flour using your fingertips until the mixture resembles fresh breadcrumbs. Stir in the sugar.
2. Pour in most of the milk, and stir using a round-bladed knife to form a soft dough, adding more of the milk if necessary.
3. Turn on to a lightly floured surface and knead gently to form a smooth ball, taking care not to over-handle.
4. Roll or press the dough out to a thickness of 2cm/¾in. Using a 6cm/2½in round cutter, stamp out 12 rounds, gently rerolling the trimmings.
5. Place the scones on a lightly greased baking sheet and brush the tops with beaten egg. Bake for 12 – 15 minutes until golden. Transfer to a wire rack to cool slightly, and then serve, split and buttered, with Bramble Jelly.

POTTED SHRIMPS

AND SALMON

Serves: 6

Preparation time: 15 minutes plus cooling and chilling

Cooking time: approx. 5 minutes

225g/8oz butter

350g/12oz peeled shrimps or small prawns, thawed if frozen

Pinch of ground mace

Pinch of cayenne pepper

Pinch of ground nutmeg

100g/4oz smoked salmon, cut into thin shreds

1. Place the butter in a small saucepan and melt over a low heat until liquid, without browning. Remove from the heat and allow to stand until the sediment sinks to the bottom, and then strain through clean muslin.

2. Reserving about a quarter of the butter, reheat the remaining over a gentle heat and add the shrimps and spices. Cook, stirring, for 2 – 3 minutes until the shrimps are well coated in the butter. Remove from the heat and cool for 10 minutes. Stir in the smoked salmon.

3. Divide between 6 small ramekin dishes or pots, pressing down lightly, and allow to cool. Poor over the remaining butter to seal the pots and chill for 1 hour. Serve with oatcakes or brown bread, and wedges of lemon to squeeze over.

SHORTBREAD

No Highland tea would be complete without shortbread. It is always made in a hand-carved wooden shortbread mould for the Royal Family.

Serves: 6

Preparation time: 15 minutes
Cooking time: approx. 45 minutes

150g/5oz plain flour
3 tbsp ground rice
50g/2oz caster sugar
100g/4oz piece of butter
Caster sugar for dredging

Preheat the oven to 170° C/325° F/Gas 3

1. Sift the flour and ground rice into a bowl and stir in the sugar. Add the butter, and, keeping it in one piece, gradually work the dry ingredients into it. Then knead until smooth.

2. Pack into a floured 20cm/8in shortbread mould and turn on to a baking sheet. Alternatively, pack into an 18cm/7in shallow cake tin and prick all over with a fork.

3. Bake in the oven for about 45 minutes until firm and pale golden. Mark into 6 triangles, if preferred, while still hot. If using a cake tin, cool for 10 minutes before turning on to a wire rack to cool.

4. When cold, dredge with caster sugar, cut into wedges and serve.

BALMORAL CASTLE

Time seems to have stood still in this turreted Royal castle which stands in an idyllic setting amidst 50,000 acres of Scottish Highlands.

Little has changed since Prince Albert constructed this romantic retreat in 1853 for Queen Victoria, and the couple spent many happy times there.

The 'VRI', the imperial crest of Queen Victoria, can still be seen on the flock wallpaper that lines the walls of the corridors and hallways, and green Hunting Stewart tartan carpet disappears into the darkness. Around every corner regiments of antlers stand guard, souvenirs of previous Royal hunting parties.

The castle and grounds are the private property of the reigning monarch, and of all the Royal households, this is the most private and special. Here, every member of the family wears a kilt as everyday attire and the men change into a 'dress' tartan kilt for dinner. Although a strict daily routine is observed, the atmosphere is relaxed and informal. This gives the Royal Family a chance to relax and enjoy the simple pleasures of country life, far removed from the formalities of their public life.

BANANA LOAF CAKE

A hearty alternative to the more traditional Dundee Cake. It is perfect for tea time.

Serves: 8 – 10

Preparation time: 15 minutes plus 24 hours storing

Cooking time: approx. 1 hour 15 minutes

75g/3oz butter, softened
175g/6oz light brown sugar
2 medium eggs
2 large bananas
200g/7oz self-raising flour
¼ tsp bicarbonate of soda
½ tsp salt
100g/4oz finely chopped walnuts
25g/1oz banana chips
25g/1oz walnut pieces

Preheat the oven to 180° C/350° F/Gas 4

1. Grease and line a 900g/2lb loaf tin. In a bowl, cream together the butter and sugar until pale and creamy. Gradually beat in the eggs.
2. Peel and mash the bananas and stir into the creamed mixture.
3. Sift the flour into the bowl with the bicarbonate of soda and salt, and add the chopped walnuts. Fold in gently and then pile into the loaf tin. Smooth over the top and arrange the banana chips on top. Sprinkle with the walnut pieces and bake for 1-1¼ hours until well risen and just firm. A skewer inserted into the centre should come out clean. Turn on to a wire rack and allow to cool.
4. Wrap the loaf in foil and keep for 24 hours before serving sliced and buttered.

RAISED CHICKEN, HAM AND MUSHROOM PIE

Serves: 6 – 8

Preparation time: 1 hour plus cooling, standing and chilling

Cooking time: approx. 2 hours 35 minutes

2 tbsp olive oil

1 medium red onion, peeled and finely chopped

1 tbsp lemon juice

150g/5oz small chestnut mushrooms, wiped and sliced

800g/1¾ lb skinless, boneless chicken breasts, finely chopped

225g/8oz lean cooked gammon, finely diced

4 tbsp freshly chopped parsley

Salt and freshly ground black pepper

FOR THE PASTRY

675g/1½lb strong plain flour

2tsp salt

75g/3oz lard or white vegetable fat

75g/3oz unsalted butter

175 ml/6 fl oz milk

1 medium egg, beaten

Preheat the oven to 200° C/400° F/Gas 6.

Grease a deep 20 cm/8in loose bottomed round cake tin.

1. Heat the oil in a frying pan and gently fry the onion with the lemon juice for 3 – 4 minutes until just softened. Add the mushrooms and cook for a further 2 – 3 minutes until the mushrooms are tender. Allow to cool then transfer to a large bowl and mix with the chicken, gammon, parsley and seasoning. Cover and chill until required.

2. Now make the pastry. Sift the flour and salt into a large heatproof bowl and rub in half the white fat. Place the remaining fat with the butter in a saucepan. Pour in the milk and 275 ml/9 fl oz water. Heat gently until the fats have melted.

3. Bring to a boil and then beat into the flour mixture. Turn on to a lightly floured surface and knead until smooth. Roll out two thirds of the pastry into a round with a thickness of 1cm/½in. Gently ease into the tin, pressing lightly to make sure the pastry fits the tin. Trim the pastry to leave a 1cm/½in over hang.

4. Pile the prepared chicken filling into the pastry case and pack down well. Fold the pastry rim over the filling and brush with beaten egg. Roll out the remaining pastry to fit the top of the pie and place on top. Using a sharp knife, score the edges of the pie to seal and then make 2 holes in the top to allow steam to escape.

5. Roll out any pastry trimmings and make leaves or other decorations for the top of the pie. Glaze the pie with egg and secure the pastry decorations to the top. Stand on a baking sheet and bake for 30 minutes. Lower the temperature to 150° C/300° F/Gas 2, reglaze the pie and cook for a further 1½ hours, covering with a layer of foil if it starts to over-brown. Cool for 20 minutes then remove from the tin. Place on a baking sheet and brush the sides of the pie with more egg. Bake for a further 20 – 25 minutes until the pie is golden. Allow to cool completely, then chill for at least 1 hour before slicing to serve.

FAMILY SUPPER

On these dark autumnal nights standing around crackling bonfires and following the firework displays, there is no better way to round off the evening than with a hearty family supper. Easy to prepare and eat, these recipes will appeal to the whole family.

PUMPKIN SOUP WITH DEVIL'S GARLIC BREAD

A tasty and delicious alternative to the usual winter warming soups. This is an excellent way of using up the pumpkin flesh left over from making your Hallowe'en lantern – (see Cook's note).

Serves: 4

Preparation time: 10 minutes
Cooking time: approx. 30 minutes

2 tbsp olive oil
1 large onion, peeled and finely chopped
425g/15oz can pumpkin purée
1 tbsp freshly chopped thyme or 1tsp dried
½ tsp ground cinnamon
½ tsp ground cumin
1tsp ground coriander
900 ml/1½ pt vegetable stock
400g/14oz can chopped tomatoes
Salt and freshly ground black pepper
Fresh thyme to garnish

FOR THE BREAD
1 x Ciabatta loaf
100g/4oz butter, softened
2 garlic cloves, peeled and crushed
1 tbsp wholegrain mustard
2 tbsp freshly grated Parmesan cheese

Preheat the oven to 200° C/400° F/Gas 6

1. For the soup, heat the oil in a large saucepan and gently fry the onion for 3 – 4 minutes until just softened but not browned.
2. Stir in the pumpkin purée, thyme, spices, stock and chopped tomatoes. Season well and bring to a boil. Simmer for 25 minutes until thick and tender. If you prefer a smooth soup, blend for a few seconds in a food processor or blender.
3. Meanwhile, make the bread. Slice the bread across at 2.5cm/1in intervals, taking care not to cut all the way through.
4. Mix the remaining ingredients together and season with black pepper. Spread in between each slice of bread. Wrap the bread in foil and bake in the oven for 20 minutes until the butter is melted and the bread is hot.
5. To serve, ladle the soup into warmed soup bowls or large mugs and serve with the hot bread. Sprinkle the soup with fresh thyme and ground pepper, if liked.

Cook's note: discard the seeds and chop the flesh of your pumpkin into small pieces. Place in a saucepan with a few tablespoons of water and bring to a boil. Cover and simmer gently for 10 – 15 minutes, adding more water if necessary, until tender. Cool and purée and use in the soup or as a filling for a pie.

PUMPKINS

The pumpkin lanterns used at Hallowe'en originated from Ireland. The labourers, returning home late from work in the fields, hollowed out turnips or beet and used them as lanterns. When Irish immigrants arrived in America they used pumpkins instead.

SPICY COTTAGE PIE

Traditionally Shepherd's Pie is made using minced lamb, and a Cottage Pie with minced beef. This is a spiced-up variation, easy to eat with a fork round the bonfire.

Serves: 4

Preparation time: 30 minutes plus cooling
Cooking time: approx. 1 hour 15 minutes

1 tbsp vegetable oil
1 medium onion, peeled and finely chopped
450g/1lb lean minced beef
½ – 1tsp hot chilli powder
1 tsp ground cumin
1 tsp dried mixed herbs
2 tbsp plain flour
300 ml/½ pt beef stock
Salt and freshly ground black pepper
425g/15oz can kidney beans, drained and rinsed

FOR THE POTATO TOPPING
900g/2lb potatoes
4 tbsp olive oil
2 garlic cloves, peeled and crushed
4 tbsp freshly chopped coriander
1 medium egg, beaten

Preheat the oven to 190° C/375° F/Gas 5

1. Heat the vegetable oil in a saucepan and gently fry the onion for 3 – 4 minutes until just softened. Add the minced beef, chilli powder to taste, cumin and herbs and cook, stirring, for 2 – 3 minutes until browned all over.

2. Stir in the flour, stock and seasoning. Bring to a boil and simmer for 15 minutes, stirring occasionally. Add the kidney beans and cook for a further 5 minutes. Transfer to a 1.5lt/2½ pt ovenproof dish and set aside to cool while preparing the topping.

3. Peel and chop the potatoes and place in a large saucepan. Cover with water and add 1tsp salt. Bring to a boil and cook for 10 – 15 minutes until tender. Drain well, return to the saucepan and mash well.

4. In a small saucepan, heat the oil until hot and fry the garlic for 30 seconds until tender – do not allow to brown. Pour into the mashed potatoes, add the chopped coriander, season and mix well. Cool for 10 minutes.

5. Pile on top of the beef mixture to cover completely. Carefully brush the top with beaten egg and bake for 20 – 25 minutes until the pie is golden.

BANANA BREAD AND BUTTER PUDDING

A traditional recipe with a Royal twist, this dish was prepared regularly at Kensington Palace and Highgrove.

Serves: 4

Preparation time: approx. 20 minutes plus 30 minutes standing
Cooking time: approx. 30 minutes

75g/3oz butter, softened
75g/3oz sultanas
1 vanilla pod
450 ml/¾ pt single cream
6 thick slices white bread
1 large banana
3 medium eggs
2 tbsp light brown sugar

Preheat the oven to 180° C/350° F/Gas 4

1. Using a little of the butter, grease an ovenproof gratin dish. Sprinkle half the sultanas over the bottom.

2. Split the vanilla pod down the middle and scrape the seeds into a saucepan. Add the pod and pour in the cream. Heat until just about to boil then remove from the heat and stand for 30 minutes.

3. Meanwhile, spread the bread thickly with remaining butter and then cut in half diagonally. Peel and finely slice the banana and arrange on 6 pieces of bread. Sandwich with remaining bread and cut in half again. Arrange, overlapping, in the prepared dish.

4. Whisk together the eggs and sugar until pale and frothy, and pour the cream through a sieve over the eggs. Pour over the bread, and sprinkle the remaining sultanas over the top.

5. Place the gratin dish in a roasting tin and pour sufficient boiling water into the roasting tin to come halfway up the side of the gratin dish. Bake for 30 – 35 minutes until the blade of a small knife inserted into the centre of the pudding comes out clean. Serve hot with pouring cream.

HIGHGROVE HOUSE

The Prince of Wales bought this listed Georgian country house in 1980. Nestling in the foothills of the Cotswolds in Gloucestershire, he intended it to be his country retreat for himself and his then future wife, Lady Diana Spencer.

Over the years, the couple took a great interest in the development of Highgrove, and it became an invaluable retreat for them and their family.

The three-storey house acquired a nursery and two guest suites for weekend entertaining. Outside in the grounds, several acres of garden, including a magnificently restored Victorian walled kitchen garden, have been developed into a well-planned and beautiful hideaway for the Prince of Wales and his sons.

STICKY GINGER AND ORANGE BAT CAKES

A variation of Parkin, a gingery, treacle cake from the north of England, which will be popular with children of all ages.

Makes: 12
Preparation time: 20 minutes plus cooling and setting
Cooking time: approx. 50 minutes

100g/4oz black treacle/molasses
100g/4oz golden syrup
100g/4oz dark muscavado sugar
100g/4oz butter
225g/8oz self-raising flour
1tsp ground ginger
1tsp mixed spice
1tsp finely grated orange rind
150 ml/¼ pt + 4 – 6 tsp freshly squeezed orange juice
100g/4oz icing sugar
12 black bat jelly or gummy sweets

Preheat the oven to 160° C/325° F/Gas 3
Grease and line a 20cm/8in square cake tin.

1. Place the treacle, syrup, sugar and butter in a saucepan and heat gently until melted together.
2. Sift the flour and spices into a mixing bowl and make a well in the centre. Add the orange rind and pour in 150 ml/¼ pt orange juice, and then stir in the melted mixture to form a smooth, thick batter.
3. Pour the mixture into the prepared tin and bake for 50 minutes or until risen and firm to the touch. Leave to cool in the tin on a wire rack. Then turn out and cut into 12 equal portions, and arrange on a wire rack.
4. Sift the icing sugar into a small bowl and then add sufficient of the remaining orange juice to form a smooth, soft icing. Using a teaspoon, drizzle the icing over each piece of cake, and top each piece with a bat sweet. Stand for 15 minutes to set before serving.

Cook's note: if you prefer, you can make edible bats for decoration from a small piece of black fondant icing. Roll out the fondant thinly on a surface lightly dusted with icing sugar, and cut out 12 small bat shapes using a cutter or template. Place on the ginger cake before the icing sets.

HALLOWE'EN AND GUY FAWKES NIGHT

In the UK the celebration of Hallowe'en derives from the tradition of Hallowtide, a two-day feast linking the eve of All Saints' Day (1 November) to All Souls' Day (2 November). The early Christian church incorporated the great pagan feast of Samhain, which marked the end of the summer and autumnal season and the onset of winter – the time when the dead were believed to return to walk the earth and bring evil with them.

Fires were lit to keep them away, and much drinking, dancing and feasting took place, and sometimes human sacrifices were made.

The Church disapproved of this and the feast of All Souls' was adapted to remember the dead and to pray for the souls in Purgatory.

Soon human sacrifice gave way to bonfire effigies. One, Shandy Dan, was held at Balmoral, and was enjoyed by Queen Victoria. Games became harmless rituals – bobbing apples for example. Bands of young men visited neighbours and friends wearing masks and odd clothes. Soul-cake, a warm currant cake, was handed out to the men as they passed by.

This ancient ceremony links effortlessly with Guy Fawkes Night. Fawkes, a Catholic, was the active member of a plot to blow up the Houses of Parliament on 5 November 1605. A small band headed by Robert Catesby arranged with Fawkes to place barrels of gunpowder in a cellar underneath the parliament buildings.

One conspirator, however, sent a letter to a friend saying that 'parliament would suffer a blow from which it could not recover'. The letter was given to James I, who deduced that gunpowder was intended. He ordered the cellars to be searched and Fawkes was discovered.

Fawkes was tortured, hung, drawn and quartered, but his name lives on with the effigies which are burnt on bonfires at the celebrations held on or near 5 November. To all this has been grafted the American custom of Hallowe'en, which in Britain takes the form of children visiting houses and demanding 'trick or treat'.

SPOOKY JACKET POTATOES

For an alternative to serve with the soup, bake medium-sized potatoes in their skins and then cut in half. Scoop out the potato flesh into a bowl and mash with a knob of butter and a little milk or cream. Season and then pile back into the potato shells. Smooth the surface of the potatoes and then squeeze the potato halves about one third of the way down so that a slight dent forms in each side. Decorate this end of the potato with small pieces of black olive to look like eyes and a mouth and return to the oven at a low heat to keep warm until ready to serve.

Winter

WINTER

Christmas is the most magical and exciting time of year. The celebration of the birth of Jesus is the time when families come together to exchange gifts, enjoy each other's company and eat, drink and generally be very merry! For me, Christmas conjures up memories of excitement and anticipation. It was instilled in my two younger brothers and me that Father Christmas would only come when we were asleep.

For many years, the Queen traditionally spent the festive season at Windsor Castle, as it could easily accommodate her ever-growing family.

My first-ever duty as a young footman back in 1976 was to serve coffee to the Queen at dinner on Christmas Eve in the State dining room of Windsor Castle. Imagine the scene: the entire Royal Family sitting around a huge polished table and an unfamiliar, very nervous eighteen-year-old boy crosses the room with a tray of rattling coffee cups. I was absolutely terrified, but it was a situation I soon became accustomed to.

After Christmas the Royal Family would move to Sandringham House, the Queen's private home in Norfolk, for the New Year celebrations. However, in recent years, Sandringham has become their home for the entire Christmas and New Year period. The family can be seen attending church on Christmas morning at the small parish church within walking distance of Sandringham House.

Christmas at Kensington Palace was entirely different. It was always the Princess's wish for her boys to experience this special time of the year with their father, grandparents, aunts, uncles and cousins. She chose to spend Christmas alone, although on one memorable occasion it was spent in the company of the entire Kensington and Chelsea Fire Brigade as her scented candles accidentally triggered off the fire alarms!

I have chosen a Victorian theme for my Christmas menu, as it was the Victorians who established most of the traditions that we are familiar with today. Whatever your taste, the following chapter will, I hope, provide you with the inspiration to make this coming Christmas and New Year an enjoyable and truly memorable one.

THE MAGIC OF CHRISTMAS

Christmas is a combination of festivals and traditions which can be traced back to the Roman invasion of Britain, when they bought with them their teachings of Christianity. Aspects of Pagan festivals and Druid traditions have all been absorbed into our Christmas culture. For example, Juul, a Viking winter festival in honour of their God, Odin, is where the word 'Yule' originates, and Pagan rituals included decking houses with greenery to give a safe haven for winter spirits. The Romans decorated their homes with swags of holly to celebrate the New Year, and the Anglo-Saxons incorporated mistletoe into their decorations, believing that it protected their homes against witchcraft.

The tradition of Father Christmas was introduced to us by our American cousins. St Nicholas was a bishop in Asia Minor and he was particularly kind to children and showed great interest in their welfare. According to legend, he threw three bags of gold through the window of a poor family and each bag fell into a stocking of the young girls within as they were hung up to dry over the fireplace.

Thus the tradition of Christmas stockings was adopted by the early Dutch settlers who founded New York. The ideals of 'Sinter Klaas' who became Santa Claus have since melted into our culture and are now commonplace.

The giving of presents on Christmas Eve was a tradition that began in Victorian times and, by the end of the 19th century, Christmas was almost as traditional as it is today. Previously, presents were exchanged on St Nicholas' Day (6 December) or at the New Year. The Royal Family open their presents after tea on Christmas Eve. Christmas stockings are, however, reserved for Christmas morning and are still filled by members of the Royal Family for their children.

A CHRISTMAS WREATH
FOR YOUR DOOR

What could provide a more festive welcome than this natural Christmas decoration to greet your friends and family as they enter your home? The beauty of this design is that it can also be used as the basis for a table decoration – simply place on a board and fill the centre with three ivory candles of varying heights. Before you begin to assemble the Christmas wreath, map out on a piece of paper exactly where each item is to be placed. Arrange decorative items in groups of 3s, 5s and 7s, and don't be afraid to put things in pairs – this can only enhance the visual impact. Once Christmas is over you can put the wreath out in the garden for the birds to eat.

5.

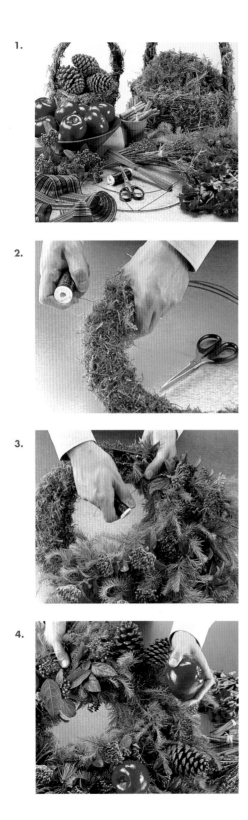

1.

2.

3.

4.

Step 1

    1 carrier bag full of sphagnum moss

    23cm/9in wire ring (available from florists)

    1 spool of reel wire

    Small branches of larch fern or other evergreen

    Small stems of viburnum or ivy

    A few lengths of stub wire

    5 large fir cones

    5 red apples

    5 bundles of dried lavender

    3 bundles of dried red roses

    5 bundles of cinnamon sticks

    Approx. 4m/12 feet length of wide tartan ribbon

Step 2

Pack small bunches of moss firmly into the ring. At the same time, wind round the reel wire to hold the moss in place. Trim the moss neatly using a pair of scissors.

Step 3

To attach the fern to the moss ring, bunch pieces of fern and viburnum (or ivy) together at angles, then carefully attach to the moss ring by winding the reel wire around each bundle. Continue until the fern is completely covering the ring of moss.

Step 4

Attach the trimmings to the ring using short lengths of stub wire. Wind a piece round the base of each fir cone and twist, making sure there is sufficient wire left on each side to wrap around the ring. Skewer the apples with the wire, through their base, and twist the ends of the wire together. Wire up the small bundles of lavender, cinnamon and dried roses. Secure the fir cones to the ring, followed by the apples and finally the small wired-up bundles.

Step 5

To complete the wreath, wind some stub wire through the top back part of the wreath and twist the ends together to form a hook. At the opposite end, tie the ribbon round in a large bow, and allow the ends to drape down

CHRISTMAS LUNCH

Christmas would not be complete without a turkey or Christmas pudding. Turkeys are indigenous to North America, and the Pilgrim Fathers served turkey at their inaugural Thanksgiving Day service in 1621. The turkey has largely replaced the Victorian tradition of roast goose. Working-class Victorians would pay into a 'goose club', usually run by the local publican on a weekly basis. By the end of the year enough money would have been saved to provide the family with a plump goose for Christmas lunch. I have decided to restore the tradition with a delicious recipe for roast goose as part of my interpretation of a traditional Christmas menu.

ROSEMARY BREAD CASES WITH FENNEL AND EGG FRICASSEE

This particular favourite is an ideal first course for any occasion but especially at Christmas. Rosemary bread is an excellent and tasty alternative and complements the light egg fricassee.

Serves: 8

Preparation time: 20 minutes
Cooking time: approx. 33 minutes

8 large thin slices white bread
175g/6oz butter
2 tbsp freshly chopped rosemary or 2 tsp dried
3 medium eggs
1 small bulb fennel
2 tbsp single cream
2 plum tomatoes, skinned, seeded and finely diced
Fresh rosemary to garnish

Preheat the oven to 200° C/400° F/Gas 6

1. Remove the crusts from the bread, and roll each slice lightly with a rolling pin to flatten slightly.
2. Melt 100g/4oz butter and lightly brush some into 8 deep muffin tins. Add the chopped rosemary to the remaining melted butter.
3. Press a bread slice into each tin and then brush generously with the rosemary butter. Season and bake in the oven for 10 minutes. Stand for 10 minutes, then remove from the tins, place on a baking tray and cook for a further 5 – 6 minutes until golden and crisp. Keep warm.
4. Place the eggs in a saucepan and cover with water. Bring to a boil and cook for 8 minutes. Drain well and cool under cold running water. Then peel and chop.
5. Trim and reserve any fronds from the fennel. Discard any damaged outer layers, and then finely slice the white flesh.
6. Melt the remaining butter and gently fry the fennel for 5 minutes until just softened. Add the chopped eggs and cream, and season. Cook, stirring, for a further minute until hot.
7. Pile the mixture into each bread case, and serve whilst warm with chopped fresh tomato and garnished with reserved fennel fronds and fresh rosemary. Season with black pepper .

The largest Christmas turkey bred in Britain was one which finally weighed 86lb. It was sold for £4,400 at a charity auction in 1989.

Tom Smith was the inventor of the Christmas cracker in the middle of the 19th century.
It is now an essential part of the festivities and can provide an extra element of colour on the Christmas table.

ROAST GOOSE WITH BAKED APPLES AND SAGE AND ONION STUFFING

I have decided to restore the tradition and show you a delicious recipe for Roast Goose with Sage and Onion Stuffing, as part of my interpretation of a traditional Christmas menu

Serves: 8

Preparation time: 45 minutes plus cooling

Cooking time: approx. 3 hours 15 minutes

5 medium onions

4 tbsp freshly chopped sage or 1 tbsp dried

175g/6oz fresh white breadcrumbs

75g/3oz butter

Salt and freshly ground black pepper

4 – 5 kg/9 – 11lb oven-ready goose, giblets removed

50g/2oz no-need-to-soak dried apricots, finely chopped

25g/1oz raisins, chopped

25g/1oz walnuts, chopped

1 tsp ground cinnamon

8 small cooking apples

Fresh sage to garnish

Preheat the oven to 200° C/400° F/Gas 6

The first Christmas cards were commissioned and sent by Henry Cole, the founder of the Victoria and Albert Museum, in 1846. However, it wasn't until 1870 that the exchanging of cards became popular with the introduction of a cheaper rate of postage.

1. First make the stuffing. Peel and roughly chop 4 of the onions, place in a saucepan and pour over 600 ml/1 pt water. Bring to a boil and simmer for 10 minutes until very soft. Then drain well and blend in a food processor until smooth or push through a sieve into a bowl to form a purée.

2. Transfer to a large bowl and stir in the sage and breadcrumbs. Melt 50g/2oz butter and stir into the mixture. Season well and allow to cool.

3. Next prepare the goose. Pull out the fat from inside the goose cavity and set aside. Prick the skin all over with a fork and then rub with salt.

4. Spoon the cooled stuffing into the neck cavity of the goose. Any left-over stuffing can be baked alongside the goose in a buttered dish for the last 30 minutes of cooking time. Skewer the neck skin to the back of the bird, and then truss and tie up with string. Weigh the bird and calculate the cooking time at 15 minutes per 450g/1lb plus an extra 15 minutes.

5. Place the goose on a wire rack above a roasting tin. Cover the breast with the reserved goose fat, and then cover with foil. Bake in the oven for the required time, basting frequently. Remove the foil for the last 30 minutes to allow the goose to brown.

6. For the baked apples, peel and finely chop the remaining onion, melt the remaining butter and gently fry the onion for 5 minutes until soft. Remove from the heat and stir in the apricots, raisins, walnuts, cinnamon and seasoning.

7. Core the apples and score the skin around the middle of each. Press the fruity filling into each apple, and place in a baking dish. Place in the oven to cook for the last 30 minutes of roasting time.

8. Once the goose is cooked, drain and place on a warmed serving platter. Allow to stand for 15 minutes. Arrange the baked apples around the goose, and garnish with fresh sage. Serve with redcurrant jelly.

Cook's tip: to test to see if the goose is cooked, pierce with a skewer in the thickest part of the leg. If the juices run clear the bird is cooked.

TIPSY RATAFIA TRIFLE

Everyone is familiar with the fruited Christmas Pudding which for some is a rather heavy conclusion to an already rich meal. This traditional Victorian alternative combines the fresh taste of fruit with sweet dessert wine to give it a modern twist. It is an excellent alternative and one which will be popular with all members of your family. It can be made a few hours in advance and will keep for 3 – 4 days.

Serves: 8
Preparation time: 15 minutes plus soaking and chilling
No cooking

6 almond macaroons
2 tbsp raspberry jam
40 ratafia biscuits
4 tbsp dessert wine or sweet sherry
4 tbsp brandy
225g/8oz raspberries, thawed if frozen
4 slices pineapple, peeled and cut into small pieces
1 quantity of *Crème Anglaise* (see page 54) or
750 ml/1¼ pt good-quality custard sauce
600 ml/1 pt whipping cream
Gold dragees and frosted rose petals to decorate

1. Spread the macaroons with raspberry jam and place jam side up in the base of a glass serving bowl. Top with the ratafias and spoon over the wine or sherry and brandy. Set aside to soak for 1 hour.

2. Spoon over the raspberries and pineapple, and pour over the *Crème Anglaise* or custard sauce. Whip the cream until just peaking and pile over the top. Cover and chill for 30 minutes.

3. Serve decorated with dragees and frosted rose petals.

Cook's note: to frost rose petals, wash and dry a few rose petals. Lightly beat an egg white until frothy and dip the petals. Shake off any excess liquid and then sprinkle with caster sugar. Place on sheets of greaseproof paper to dry.

SANDRINGHAM HOUSE

This red-brick, multi-faceted Edwardian building resembles a rather grand shooting lodge. The house has a baronial central hall complete with minstrel gallery, hanging tapestries and an eight-foot-square fireplace. Large house parties, especially shooting parties, can easily be accommodated within its panelled interior.
The Royal Family traditionally spend the festive season here and their daily life is punctuated with shoots, lunches and dinner parties.

Although Queen Victoria preferred the vacational atmosphere of Osborne House on the Isle of Wight, her son Edward VII regularly entertained at Sandringham House. The *Daily Sketch* reported in December 1914 that the Christmas menu at Sandringham would be turkey, goose, baron of beef, pork, cygnet from the Thames, boar's head, mince pies and a flaming plum pudding, 'which will be carved by the King'. The tenants would have venison given them from the estate.

Later Queen Adelaide, the wife of William IV, made a large fir tree lit with candles the centre of her Christmas drawing room and this custom was followed in the household of Princess Victoria at Kensington Palace. After her marriage, the Royal Household had several Christmas trees for the Queen, her consort and each of the children. Each of the ladies-in-waiting was also given one. All were lit on Christmas Eve when the presents were given out. Afterwards the candles were put out and not lit again until the evening of Christmas Day. The tallest tree was always placed in the drawing room where the candles could be relit when required, especially on New Year's Eve and Twelfth Night.

Although Prince Albert was once credited with bringing the first Christmas tree to Britain, it is now accepted that the Prince made the custom popular as the centrepiece of Christmas festivities. There is a reference to Princess Mary, daughter of Henry VIII, later Mary I, having one Christmas a rosemary bush spangled with gold.

The first mention of a decorated tree, similar to the modern one, is in 1800 when Queen Charlotte, wife of George III, had one at court. The custom came from Germany. Before her marriage Queen Charlotte was the German Princess of Mecklenburg-Strelitz. Martin Luther, the religious reformer, is said to have instigated the custom of Christmas trees in Germany and if so, he was adapting a far older tradition of bringing in greenery from the wood to neutralize the pagan worship of tree spirits.

Candles are an essential and traditional element of my Christmas decorations. Use them liberally throughout your home for illumination and a stunning display. Nothing compares to the rich, warm glow of candlelight. It will enhance the atmosphere in any room or at any table.

Create your own individual atmosphere and mood by experimenting with burning essences.

Cinnamon and jasmine have become popular and can enhance any special occasion. I would often use evaporating oils, incense sticks, burning essences and perfumed candles throughout Kensington Palace to create a special and welcoming environment in which guests would feel at ease.

Some fragrances are said to have particular qualities:

AMBERGRIS increases passion and virility
BERGAMOT aids love
CAMOMILE helps encourage calmness and tranquillity
CINNAMON provides harmony and peacefulness
LILY OF THE VALLEY soothing and calming
SANDALWOOD helps concentration and meditation

Standing guard at the doorway of the Princess's apartment, this hand-crafted nutcracker soldier always added to the spirit of Christmas.

Short of ideas for a Christmas present for me and my family one year, the Princess thought we should have something that was a special memento that no Christmas would be complete without. So she gave us this beautiful traditional crib which, every year, we assemble as a family. However the baby Jesus is not put in to his manger until Christmas morning.

This Christmas garland, hanging over the front door of the Princess's apartment at Kensington Palace, was a warm welcome for any visitor.

The Princess was overwhelmingly generous. We would select, buy, wrap and despatch approximately 150 presents each year to family and friends. Each would be accompanied by a handwritten message and a Christmas card. Every package was wrapped with loving care, with the knowledge that it would be received with great excitement. The whole event was arranged with military precision, but it was obvious to me that it was a very important time of the year for the Princess. A time to say thank you and send every possible good wish for the coming year.

Christmas paper can often be very expensive and it is much more fun designing your own exclusive individual paper. The thought of the song lyric 'brown paper packages

Presents often sit underneath the Christmas tree for weeks before they are opened. Therefore, presentation and a little imagination are very important.

tied up with string' gave me the inspiration to explore ideas with raffia bows, thick string and different coloured wools and twines. You can print traditional designs on to paper and carry the colour theme through with the ribbon and tag. Use baubles, beads, feathers and silk flowers to give the tied bow an added dimension. Let your imagination run riot!

NEW YEAR'S DRINKS AND CANAPE PARTY

With the prospect of a New Year ahead and the inevitable reflection of the year just passed, I have often found this time of year to carry with it a mixed bag of emotions. Our thoughts drift to memories of those who are no longer with us and memories of passed New Years. However, this is also a strong and positive time: the birth of something new, and an excellent time to make resolutions for the coming year.

At the stroke of midnight, amongst the renditions of *Auld Lang Syne* why not celebrate in style and raise a glass of champagne with those you love the most, and if you intend to celebrate in style at home with friends or family the catering of such an important occasion is a priority.

GRISSINI WITH CHEESE AND HAM

Breadsticks are everybody's favourite dipper. This is an interesting twist, serving them complete with dip.

Makes: 40
Preparation time: approx. 30 minutes
No cooking

150g/5oz thin-sliced Parma ham
225g/8oz soft cheese with garlic and herbs
8 tbsp natural fromage frais
Salt and freshly ground black pepper
40 Grissini breadsticks
2 tbsp poppy seeds
2 tbsp toasted sesame seeds
2 tbsp parsley

1. Trim the excess fat from the ham and then cut into thin lengthwise strips using scissors and set aside. In a bowl, beat the soft cheese to soften it and mix in the fromage frais and seasoning.

2. Taking each breadstick separately, lightly spread about 7cm/3in at the end with the cheese mixture and wind a strip or two of ham around. Stand upright in a tall wide glass whilst preparing the others.

3. Once all the sticks are covered, dip the ham end of each stick in the remaining cheese and then dip in either poppy or sesame seeds, or chopped parsley, and serve from coloured plastic or glass beakers. Do note that these sticks will go soggy if left standing for too long.

Cook's note: for a vegetarian version, simply omit the ham and dip the cheese-coated sticks in seeds or crushed salted cashew nuts or pecans.

MINI BEEF WELLINGTONS

These little parcels of succulent beef are best served straight from the oven, but they can be prepared a few hours in advance and then cooked just before serving.

Makes: 20
Preparation time: 30 minutes
Cooking time: approx. 30 minutes

350g/12oz puff pastry, thawed if frozen
350g/12oz piece lean beef fillet
Salt and freshly ground black pepper
2 tsp wholegrain mustard
2 tsp creamed horseradish
100g/4oz coarse pâté
1 medium egg, beaten

Preheat the oven to 200° C/400° F/Gas 6

1. Roll out the pastry on a lightly floured surface to a 38cm/15in square, and divide into 20 equal pieces. Cut the fillet into 20 equal portions and season well all over. Lay a piece in the centre of each pastry square.
2. Mix the mustard and horseradish together and spoon a little over each steak. Soften the pâté and press a piece on top of each steak.
3. Fold the sides of pastry up and over the meat, like an envelope, pressing down well to seal. Score the pastry diagonally and transfer to a large baking sheet. Brush with egg and bake for 25 – 30 minutes until golden and crisp. Serve immediately accompanied with a bowl of mustard and a bowl of horseradish to dip.

HISTORY OF BEEF WELLINGTON

The Duke of Wellington, who won the Battle of Waterloo in 1815, was quite indifferent to food, so much so that his cooks often gave notice, despairing of using their culinary talents in his household. In spite of this, his name has been given to a fillet of beef, wrapped in puff pastry, so called perhaps because in its larger version the finished product looks like a highly polished riding or wellington boot.

THAI-STYLE CHICKEN
AND PEPPER SATAY

Makes: 20

Preparation time: 50 minutes plus marinating

Cooking time: approx. 14 minutes

675g/1½lb skinless boneless chicken breasts

1 garlic clove, peeled and crushed

2.5cm/1in piece root ginger, peeled and grated

2 tbsp crunchy peanut butter

4 tbsp canned coconut milk

½ tsp hot chilli powder

Finely grated rind and juice of 1 lime

4 tbsp freshly chopped coriander

1 tbsp fish sauce (nam pla)

1 large red pepper

1. Cut the chicken into small chunks approx 1cm/½in thick and place in a shallow dish.

2. Mix together the remaining ingredients except the red pepper and toss with the chicken. Cover and chill for 1 hour for the flavours to develop. Meanwhile, soak 20 wooden skewers in warm water until the chicken is ready.

3. Halve and deseed the pepper and cut into small pieces about the same size as the chicken. Drain the cocktail sticks and thread pieces of chicken and pepper on to each skewer. You should have enough for 20 sticks.

4. Preheat the grill to a medium/hot setting. Arrange the skewers on a grill rack – you may need to cook them in two batches – and cook for 6 – 7 minutes, turning after 3 minutes, until tender and cooked through. Drain and serve hot or cold accompanied with satay sauce to dip.

Cook's note: if you want to make mini skewers, there will be sufficient mixture for 40 cocktail sticks. You can thread up the skewers a few hours before your guests arrive, and then grill them just before serving.

SATAY SAUCE

For an easy satay sauce, blend together 300 ml/½ pt canned coconut milk, 4 tbsp crunchy peanut butter and 1 tbsp light brown sugar. Heat 1 tsp vegetable oil in a small saucepan and gently fry 2 cloves of crushed garlic for 1 minute until softened. Stir in 1 tsp each of ground coriander and ground cumin, and a pinch of hot chilli powder, along with the coconut mixture. Bring to a boil, stirring, and simmer for 5 minutes until thickened. Remove from the heat and stir in 2 tbsp dark soy sauce and 2 tsp sesame oil. Serve hot or cold.

PRAWNS ON PARADE

This stunning dish will be a luxurious treat for your guests and it is incredibly easy to put together. Serving the prawns on crushed ice will help keep them cool.

Serves: 20

Preparation time: 15 minutes plus chilling

No cooking

40 large whole prawns such as Langoustines

4 tbsp olive oil

2 garlic cloves, peeled and crushed

Finely grated rind and juice of 1 lemon

FOR THE MAYONNAISE

300 ml/½ pt good-quality mayonnaise

2 tbsp olive oil

2 garlic cloves, peeled and crushed

Freshly ground black pepper

A few fresh basil leaves, finely shredded

½ tsp finely grated lemon rind

1. Wash, scrub and pat dry the prawns and place in a large bowl. Toss in the olive oil, garlic and lemon rind and juice. Cover and chill for 1 – 2 hours to allow the flavours to develop.

2. Meanwhile, mix all the mayonnaise ingredients together, cover and chill until required.

3. When ready to serve, pile some crushed ice on to a large platter. Drain the prawns and arrange side by side on the ice.

4. Serve the prawns immediately, accompanied with lemon wedges and the mayonnaise to dip.

Cook's note: for advice on how to tackle whole prawns, see How to Eat Difficult Food on page 21. Don't forget to provide bowls for the prawn shells and finger bowls and napkins for your guests to clean up.

ANTIPASTO AND TORTELLINI KEBABS

A continental snack which is easy to make and serve. They can be prepared well in advance and are suitable for any cocktail party or reception.

Makes: 20

Preparation time: 30 minutes plus cooling

Cooking time: approx. 5 minutes

60 pieces fresh white tortellini pasta

60 pieces fresh green tortellini pasta

Pinch of salt

1 tbsp olive oil

20 marinated artichoke hearts, drained

40 marinated pitted black olives, drained

20 sundried tomato halves in oil, drained and cut in half

A handful of small fresh basil leaves

1. Bring a saucepan of lightly salted water to the boil and cook the tortellini according to the packet instructions. Drain well and toss in the olive oil, and allow to cool.

2. Thread 6 pieces of cooked tortellini on to 20 skewers, alternating with the remaining ingredients, cover and chill until required.

CHOCOLATE RUM TRUFFLES

Serve these decadent truffles with fresh fruit to complement their richness.

Makes: 40

Preparation time: 55 minutes plus overnight chilling and setting
Cooking time: approx. 20 minutes melting

275g/9oz plain chocolate, broken into small pieces
225 ml/8 fl oz extra-thick double cream
40g/1½oz unsalted butter
2½ tbsp dark rum
1½ tbsp crème fraîche

FOR THE COATING
175g/6oz white chocolate, broken into small pieces
2 tbsp finely chopped natural pistachio nuts
175g/6oz plain chocolate, broken into small pieces
175g/6oz milk chocolate, broken into small pieces

NEW YEAR'S EVE CELEBRATIONS

Each New Year's Eve at Sandringham, the youngest and darkest haired footman would be selected to perform 'First Footing'.
The Scottish tradition is still observed by the Royal Family every year, when at the stroke of midnight, he would approach the oak front door, knock and say 'Old year out, new year in, open the door and let me in.'
Weaving his way through the entire Royal Family, he would then place another log on the open fire and present each of the Royal ladies with a small gift to which a piece of coal had been attached for good luck. His reward? A glass of champagne or mulled wine and the opportunity to wish his Employer and her family a happy New Year.

1. First make the truffle filling. Place the plain chocolate pieces in a saucepan along with the extra-thick double cream and butter. Cook, over a gentle heat, until melted, then remove from the heat and whisk in the rum and crème fraîche.

2. Line a mixing bowl with clear wrap and pour the chocolate mixture into it. Allow to cool completely, then cover and chill for a few hours or overnight until firm.

3. Turn the chilled filling out and discard the clear wrap. Divide the mixture into 40 small pieces. Working quickly, form each piece into a round and place on a tray lined with baking parchment – you may find this easier if you dust your hands with a little cocoa powder. Chill for 30 minutes.

4. For the coatings, place the white chocolate in a small heatproof bowl over a saucepan of gently simmering water and cook until melted. Remove from the heat and cool for 10 minutes. Spike one of the truffles with a skewer and spoon the melted chocolate over until it is covered. Place on a sheet of baking parchment whilst preparing another 12 truffles. Sprinkle each with a little pinch of chopped nuts and chill until set.

5. Repeat this with the plain chocolate, coating another 13 truffles. Finally, melt the milk chocolate and coat the remaining truffles.

6. Leave the truffles until completely set and then transfer them to a serving platter. Accompany with fresh fruit.

MINI FRUIT SKEWERS

It's nice to serve chocolate with some fruit, and a colourful way to do this is to thread small pieces of assorted fruits on to cocktail sticks and serve as mini kebabs. Kiwi fruit, melon, apples, pears, small bananas, pineapple, peaches, mandarin segments, strawberries and small grapes are popular and are easy to prepare. Try marinating the fruit first either in alcohol such as brandy, rum or Kirsch, or in fruit juice such as sieved passion fruit juice, or lime juice. Don't forget to toss fruits which discolour like apples, pears and banana in lemon juice to help prevent this. The skewers can be prepared a few hours in advance, covered and kept in the fridge until required.

COCKTAILS

A cocktail is a mixed drink with a spirit base which is traditionally served before the sun goes down. I believe the word 'cocktail' is derived from the story of the quills of rooster feathers being used aboard the Mississippi steamboats to stir the drinks served to the gamblers.

Cocktails were at their most popular during the 1920s and 1930s, ironically as prohibition hit America. Although many of their names belong to a bygone era, cocktails have regained their attraction in recent years. Professionally trained bartenders, whether at the Carlysle in Manhattan or the American Bar at the Savoy Hotel, London, still serve a mouth-watering selection.

There is something rather decadent and yet attractive about the cocktail hour. Visions of men in black ties and ladies wearing spectacular gowns come to mind. Even Scarlett O'Hara can be witnessed sipping a Mint Julep in *Gone With the Wind*. This concoction of sugar syrup mixed with bourbon and garnished with mint is still served today, and is traditionally linked with the Kentucky Derby.

COCKTAIL ORIGINS

1 May 1851	The first Cocktail Bar opened at Gore House, North Hyde Park.
1860	The first Martini was served at the Occidental Hotel, San Francisco.
1920	The Bloody Mary was invented. It was originally called Bucket of Blood, and was created at Harry's New York Bar in Paris.
1953	James Bond drinks his first Vodka Martini in the first Bond book, *Casino Royale*, by Ian Fleming.

MAKING YOUR OWN COCKTAILS

Here are two recipes for the most popular and well-known cocktails in the world – a good way to start mixing your own.

ROYAL MARTINI COCKTAIL

Made the traditional way with a gin base, and stirred, not shaken!

1. Half fill a large glass jug with ice.
2. Pour over half a bottle of gin and stir vigorously to chill the alcohol.
3. Add one dash of Dry Vermouth and several strips of lemon zest.
4. Stir vigorously and serve in Martini glasses with an ice cube and a strip of lemon zest if preferred.

Cocktail notes:
- Don't freeze the gin before making the Martini as the flavour and bouquet will be inferior.
- Try replacing the gin with vodka and serve with a green olive.
- If you serve the Martini with black olives, it becomes a Dirty Martini; and if your guests want their Martini 'straight up', serve it to them with no ice, lemon zest or olive.

SINGAPORE SLING

This quintessential tropical concoction is associated with Sir Thomas Stamford Raffles, who persuaded the East India Company to sign a treaty with the Sultan of Johore in 1819. The historic treaty turned the quiet port of Singapore into a thriving centre of commerce for British colonial activity. Singapore became a Crown Colony in 1867.

The Raffles Hotel in Singapore, where the cocktail was invented, is one of the most distinguished relics of the British Empire.

1. Shake the juice of half a lemon with 1 tsp icing or powdered sugar and 50 ml/2 fl oz gin.
2. Pile some ice cubes into a highball tumbler and strain the juice into the glass.
3. Fill the glass with soda water almost to the top.
4. Gently pour over 15 ml/1 tbsp cherry brandy. Decorate with an 'umbrella' of seasonal fruits and some straws.

The Screwdriver was invented by American oil riggers who mixed vodka and orange juice. They stirred it with the first implement which came to hand, hence the name.

ACKNOWLEDGEMENTS

I have many people to thank for their advice, assistance and friendship in putting this book together, from when it was merely a 'seed' in my mind right through the writing and production processes. It would take up too many pages to name them all, but there are a few individuals I would particularly like to mention.

Kathryn Hawkins, for her brilliant food styling and unique food knowledge; Simon Smith, for his stunning photographs and incredible patience; Clare Louise Hunt, for her exquisite taste and styling; Stephen Seedhouse, for his unparalleled knowledge of flowers; Catherine Walker, for her elegant sketch and for being my friend for many years; Bryan Adams, my friend whose music kept us sane during the photographic shoot; Katrina, Bobby, Vicky, Sue and Anthony from DW Design for their vision and interpretation of the manuscript.

I would also like to thank Asprey & Garrard, Thomas Goode and Divertimenti, whose unmistakable style is evident throughout the book.

Thanks also to Jacqueline Allen, Jane Harris, Jo Greenstead, Vanessa Corringham and Amanda Clow, my friends from Kensington Palace and the Diana, Princess of Wales Memorial Fund, who encouraged me to put my thoughts down on paper in the very early days.

Finally, thanks to my agent, Neil Reading, for protecting me from the good, the bad and the ugly (he knows exactly who I mean!); Tim Forrester and Nigel Stoneman from André Deutsch for all they have done to make this project such an enjoyable one; my editor, Louise Dixon, for her constant support and encouragement; John Aherne of Warner Books for his transatlantic guidance and support; Carol Wallace for her professional advice; and my niece, Louise Cosgrove, for all her hard work and enthusiasm – and for having faith in her old 'Unc'.

INDEX